A
WOMAN'S GUIDE
TO
MANAGING
MEN

A WOMAN'S GUIDE TO MANAGING MEN

BY

VICKY HIBBERT
AND SUE BAKER

Foreword by Vicky Wright, Managing Director,
Hay Management Consultants

BOWERDEAN PUBLISHING COMPANY LIMITED

First published in 1995 by the Bowerdean Publishing Company Ltd.
of 8 Abbotstone Road, London SW15 1QR

British Library Cataloguing-in-Publication Data.
**A catalogue record for this book is available from the British
Library.**

ISBN 0 906097 19 3 Original Paperback.

Designed and typeset by the Bowerdean Publishing Company Ltd.
Printed in Great Britain by BPC Wheatons Ltd, Exeter

CONTENTS

Contents

FOREWORD

Vicky Wright, Managing Director, Hay Management Consultants Ltd.

Despite high levels of participation of women in the workforce, the majority of women who take up their first managerial appointment find themselves in an environment where most role models are men. Even when others advise that the challenges encountered by women in their new role and new relationships are those that 'everyone goes through', it is difficult not to feel that being a woman manager means there are certain different issues to be faced. These are not just personal for the new appointee – they may affect new bosses, new colleagues and those being managed. Research also shows that women managers do differ from men in their managerial approach, behaviour and attitudes. For example, a study in a regional health authority showed that the management styles used by female managers are not as effective as or visible with male subordinates as those of male counterparts. This should not surprise us – women often have different educational, career and life experience from those of their male peers.

As one of the increasing number of women in management I must confess to starting my career with some naïvety about the challenges I would face. A reasonable academic ability and a high achievement motivation easily got me on the first rungs of a career ladder. Also a sponsor in my early career who regarded fostering and shaping raw graduate talent as his job, regardless of gender, shielded me from the realitiee of the tough career I had chosen.

So it was only in mid-career that I began to ask whether enough was being, done for me and other women, to equip us better for management. It came home to me when I was asked to tutor on the Runge effective leadership campaign for the Industrial Society in the 1980s. This was the flagship management programme of its time; of the 100 or so partici-pants there were only two or three women, plus two female tutors. I was shocked.

A lot has happened since then. I should acknowledge that the Industrial Society itself did much to rectify the imbal-ance of training opportunities given by employers. But in the UK there is still a shortage of practical, well-researched material for women managers, those responsible for man-agement development and training and bosses of women managers. This is why I welcome this book based on case studies of successful women. It does not burden with theo-ry. It helps by giving insights into how women have put together the necessary stages of planning and realizing their managerial careers – and how they have overcome hurdles along the way.

This book provides many useful tips. I am sure it will also show readers that the day-to-day difficulties in furthering their careers and their relationships have tried and tested solutions. But for women managers this book has another great advantage: in many ways it is comforting to know that in some of our experiences we have not been alone.

INTRODUCTION

Redheads can't take responsibility.
The Welsh don't understand discipline.
Lefthanders can't deal with clients.

Can you imagine making a statement like that? Or even agreeing that the colour of your hair, where you were born or your dexterity made a real difference to your ability as a manager? Of course this is all nonsense – but many women suffer this type of prejudice all the time. Despite legislation for equal opportunities, against discrimination ...

Women are more emotional, aren't they?

The clichés remain. The gaps in earnings between male and female remain. In particular, the difference between the numbers of men and women getting to the top of industry and the professions stays obstinately wide. While men still retain the reins on recruitment, promotion and development, this may take many years to change.

After a quarter of a century of equal pay, even liberated daily newspapers refer to businessmen as if there were no professional women at work. Yet as many women as men graduate from medical schools and teacher training colleges.

1

Young women emerging from colleges and universities now have as high expectations for their careers as their male counterparts. They see no more reason to be held back because of their sex than because of the colour of their hair. Yet, while power is still concentrated in the hands of men with archaic attitudes, women will have to counter discrimination, covert or overt, and their entry into the workforce and their progress up the career ladder will continue to be obstructed by more and different obstacles from those faced by their male counterparts.

This book is aimed at women wanting to enter management and at managers planning to rise up through the hierarchy. It looks at the particular hazards women managers face in dealing with the male of the species in a management context and gives practical tips on how to survive and come out ahead of the competition. Some of the problems – politics, the hierarchy and the opposite sex – are common to managers of either sex, but we have approached them from the female point of view. Not just our own. We have sought the views of 26 women managers and have interviewed 20 in depth. They form an A–Z of management experience at various levels and in different industries. Their career histories are summarized in the Appendix for reference.

These women managers describe their struggles to get a job, facing mostly male interviewers and dealing with hostility from male peers, suspicion from subordinates and patronizing from male bosses. They talk about dealing with discrimination, harassment and conflict; juggling work and family life; and, finally, their ambitions. Not one is superwoman. All have spoken honestly about failures and successes. They talked about where they went wrong and how they might have handled it better. They also spoke of how they achieved success – the positive factors which worked for them.

Introduction

In each chapter we draw upon the experiences of our A–Z of women managers, in some cases augmenting and contrasting their ways of coping with text-book management solutions. The crucial difference between this book and any other 'how to be a manager' book is that related here is what women managers think and feel about the specific difficulties of managing in a (mostly) man's world.

They are not anti-men. Neither are we. We recognize the difference and in our private lives we celebrate it. But we also accept that at work the odds are still stacked against us.

Vicky Hibbert and Sue Baker. January 1995.

CHAPTER 1

GETTING THE JOB

To be successful a woman had to be much better at her job than a man – Golda Meir.

To move into a management job for the first time is to overcome the greatest hurdle. Of all managerial jobs only about 10–15% are held by women. Getting the job is usually a woman's first test in managing men. Some industries and professions are almost a male preserve: engineering for one. Others are more female friendly: publishing, personnel, media and retail for instance. However, some professions and disciplines attract equal numbers of men and women starting their careers, but provide limited opportunities for women at the top.

This chapter examines getting the job from outside and being promoted to management from within the organization.

Working in a Man's World

Women are increasingly being encouraged to study maths and science and to take jobs which have typically been 'men only', engineering and science for instance. Employers in these industries take equal opportunities more seriously now and women can be successful in them. Nevertheless it may take more than the usual amount of guts and determination to succeed.

Even if you choose a male-dominated profession or industry, you can increase your chances of success by researching where women do best. Also, who you know can help you in management. In the health service for instance, male consultants predominate but more women reach the top in paediatrics than in surgery. In engineering, law and accountancy some firms have a track record of promoting and encouraging women. Others keep a deathly hush – but if a look at the company's annual report reveals an all-male board, all-male senior management – beware or be prepared to blaze a trail where no woman has gone before. Our women managers have sometimes found it possible to storm the executive washroom in 'male chauvinist' firms but on occasion have retreated. Does it make sense to batter your head against the glass ceiling when another firm might be eager to value and pay you more?

Trailblazing can be a costly activity. On leaving university one of our managers went for an interview with a computing firm, not realizing that it was an all-male environment, rife with sexual innuendo, discrimination and harassment. She asked her interviewer how many women worked for the company but, although the answer was "very few", she persisted. "I did very much go through a crusading type of thing" she confessed, "but after a while reality sets in. I was fed up with trailblazing and I just had to get out."

However, if you are determined to move into a mostly male industry you have certain advantages. While women are in the minority they stand out and tend to be remembered at courses, conferences and selection boards. The grey suits may merge in the minds of the panel whereas your dress and jacket will be remarked on. (Trivial it may be to judge people on clothes but it happens.)

Even the most misogynist manager now pays lip service to equal opportunities. Personnel and human resources departments have been hammering into them for years the need (a) to avoid accusations of discrimination which could be costly in terms of pubic relations as well as court cases, and (b) the need to recruit the best from the widest selection of people.

Application Forms and CVs

Application forms frequently ask for marital status, age and ethnic origin in addition to other personal details. It is possible that the admission of being married, having children, being black or being over 40 can count against you. You may not even be interviewed. Sex and race legislation give some protection: you can take your case to a tribunal. Ageism is not currently a cause for legal action. Refusal to consider someone because of a disability was not legally enforced in the past despite a so-called 'quota system' although recent legislation is starting to deal with this. Some women refuse to answer personal questions on application forms – but this may result in them not even getting a proverbial foot in the door. Others have tried to overcome discrimination by using initials on the application form. Even if this were to get you to an interview, if the recruiters are anti-women the upshot is that the rejection is merely postponed. Moreover, lying on an application form could have legal consequences.

In Britain, CVs are generally short, concentrating on career history in brief, snappy points. In the USA, CVs are much longe and more detailed with wider achievements given prominence. It is not unusual to see an American CV spelling out public speaking engagements in detail as well as job responsibilities. Asian companies set great store by qualifications.

Getting Through the Management Door
Naturally, the higher the formal qualifications you have the better. But, in management, experience usually counts for more and it is this which helps most in applying for jobs and in gaining promotion.

'Experience' does not just mean working in a similar job. Experience from previous jobs, the home and school all count. Experience in one field can boost your confidence in applying in a different area. Jean today is a chief executive in a promotional body. She began as a nurse in the Royal Navy, followed by a spell in publishing after an Open University degree. The Navy was a great training ground and she had access to many formal training courses. She met a diverse range of people and that gave her a good grounding in dealing with men and developing management skills.

"The important thing is when you are nursing and you're in a ward with a load of Naval chaps, then you have to get confidence very quickly. You can either be sheepish and continually blush and be embarrassed about the whole thing or you just get on with the job. The chaps were a handful but fun. It taught me how to deal with people and to get that professional relationship working. You had to know how to control them – a type of discipline."

Anyone who has organized a household, dealt with screaming

toddlers, arranged meals, paid bills and stayed sane is by definition a time-manager, a people-manager and a task-ori-entated manager. Although this may be difficult to put across in applying for a job, it is worth remembering to boost your own confidence if you are returning to work and should at least stop you thinking of or referring to yourself as 'just a housewife'.

Anita who has two children and is now a senior manage-ment consultant, found managing men similar to managing children. "I'm not sure what is worse: an obstreperous board of directors or six to eight kids at a party. You learn when there are disagreements to get off the substance and go into the processes. It diffuses the tension." It would be highly unwise to make this comparison at an interview – but women frequently under-value experience and skills they have acquired in child rearing and the home.

Those coming from school or university could point to other types of experience: running a debating society or sports team, student union, or organizing fieldwork, help-ing with a charity. All these activities prove that you are active, involved and prepared to work with and for people. Some may demonstrate management potential if you describe them well. Experience of working in a local theatre box office in university holidays got one of our managers her first management job in theatre administration.

The Interview
It helps to research a company before the interview. Not only will this help you come to a decision, it could also set you apart from other candidates. Local librarians can be helpful if the company is well known. You could ring the company's national public relations department to ask for brochures and/or an annual report. Ask friends for contacts in the firm – do they know someone who works

there? Or someone who knows someone? A first-hand opinion may save you from disastrous mistakes. Still lingering in old-fashioned companies is the idea that you can employ women more cheaply, so find out the going rate if you can.

For most jobs, one or more of the selectors are likely to be men. Even now particularly older men are predisposed to certain clichéed prejudice about women. They may believe:
– *Women lack the ability to discipline staff:*
counter with real work experience, employees – past and present; stories of dealing with the hockey team, the dramatic society, children's parties.
– *Women are too soft:*
counter with examples of organizing peers in a team on work projects, running university projects, organizing younger siblings.
– *Women will not be accepted by clients:*
are no clients women? Sometimes selling to the opposite sex is easier.
– *Women will not be accepted by subordinates:*
tough! Have they tried? Will they leave?
– *Women lack leadership qualities:*
as did, say, Margaret Thatcher, Indira Ghandi?

Selectors may not put these points directly, so candidates need to understand male doubts, read the type of prejudice and insert the relevant, confident-sounding anecdote – if possible with humour as this relaxes people – but do not tell jokes.

Putting over your own confidence is crucial, particularly if you do not feel it. If you feel tense, refuse offers of tea or coffee (your hands might betray you, you might spill it). Take deep breaths before going in. Body language tells all – do not fold your arms or clench your fists. Try to look alert and relaxed and have some 'intelligent questions' ready to ask about long-term prospects within the firm.

It does not always help to be too eager (is she desperate?) or too confident by suggesting you have lots of other offers (she's not committed). But if you ask for a time-scale for the selection process because "there is a possibility of another firm......" it implies you may be in demand.

Two of our women managers applied for several jobs at once and found themselves being offered two. In the interview you may get a feel for the organization but most of the time the employer asks the questions rather than vice versa. So how to choose – intuition? Or by some other criterion, e.g. money?

Gail (training manager) was offered jobs in two TV companies. One firm offered her £500 a year more than the other. "They kept me waiting 45 minutes for the interview and the receptionist terrified me – all long red nails and not looking at you." The other company seemed chaotic but friendly. "People call it intuition but I think you should listen to what your internal voice says – it may be more like unconscious recognition of patterns of behaviour in your judgment of someone or an organization." She avoided the red nails.

Sarah (estate agent) was tempted by money. She applied for and was offered two jobs and took the one which offered more. She only stayed a short while. "On the first morning, I went to the ladies loos, locked myself in the cubicle and cried my eyes out because I'd realized I'd made a terrible mistake." The company's procedures were in a state of chaos. She decided to tackle the problem and put forward a strategy to the all–male management. "I was told to shut up." She then approached the other company which had offered her a job. She admitted her mistake and asked if they had anything for her. Fortunately they did. She has now progressed to be a director there.

Preparing for Promotion

Internal promotion can be the best way to ease yourself into the first managerial job of your career and to rise further from junior management. You know the firm, the culture, the people and the job better than any outside candidate. You can therefore prepare by training yourself up for the job (with the cooperation of your current boss or in your own time) and by being seen to be ready for more responsibility.

The majority of our interviewees had little management training before their promotion. Some had training in their speciality (accountancy, medicine, etc.). Others leapt at any opportunity to go on training courses, particularly public speaking courses which can build confidence and assertiveness. Frequently you can learn as much from other trainees as from the formal sessions and it helps in building up networks. Management books, either theory or case studies may help. (See our Further Reading list, page 130. In particular *Management for Results* by Peter Drucker is still considered a bible for managers. Rosabeth Moss Kanker is more woman-oriented and up-to-date. *Are You Managing?* by Peter Stemp is succinct and straightforward).

Putting Yourself Forward for Promotion

It may be necessary to stand out from the crowd, to get yourself noticed, to be considered for promotion. There is a danger that if you do not you are thought to be happy where you are. Colleagues may appear equal to you on paper, so there may be a tendency for management to promote the person who stands out in a positive way or, if the selectors are conservative, to pick your male peer "because we've always had a man in that job."

Putting yourself up for promotion can involve having to deal with sexist attitudes and discrimination from male bosses.

Sarah (estate agent) found in a previous job that men in her company were being promoted and given more responsibilities. Despite her longer service she was not offered such opportunities. When she protested at this she was offered a manager's job but without the title or the manager's usual car. She left.

She still believes that she has had to push herself forward in her new job. She took an aggressive sales approach and this did result in promotion. "I ploughed myself into my work. I had the time of my life working until goodness knows what time every evening, weekends and all the rest of it, but loving every moment of it. I got a taste of success. I found myself rapidly promoted."

Fiona (editor), too, got herself noticed. She put forward lots of ideas – new projects and different ways of organizing things – and dealt with problems as they arose. This she said put her "in the limelight". She did not do this as part of a conscious strategy. Rather she talked about what she believed in and introduced new ideas. The management liked them – and she got a promotion.

Using the Grapevine
The 'grapevine' was used to great advantage by some of our women managers in applying for promotion.

Olivia (engineer) believed that the grapevine worked for her. "I rang the department and went along informally one day and had a word about what they did and what was available. Having gone through the informal loop, I went back through personnel, did it all formally." She got the job she wanted. She recently heard about another job via the grapevine which was due to become available. "I'm one of the few to know that it is coming up and I want it to stay that way." This gave her the advantage of being able to express an interest before others found out and threw their hats in the ring.

The Promotion Interview

Women need to be assertive to convince a male interviewer or panel of their ability to do the job and to manage male subordinates – but not aggressive. However, you may know the interviewers and internal competition and so can prepare and tailor your interview according to the company style.

Being assertive is a useful skill – being aggressive does not help your cause. One who tried for a promotion but did not get it reflected: "At the interview I was too intense, aggressive and unwilling to acknowledge my shortcomings. I harangued the panel of interviewers." Another woman was appointed instead.

Networking

Increasingly popular, particularly in the USA, networking can help in internal promotions and in getting better jobs. Outplacement consultants recommend it highly for those without a job and know from surveys that it speeds up the process of finding work. Men have had old boy networks for years; women are just getting in on the act. Formal networks within an industry provide contacts who may be useful. There are networks, for instance, for women in banking, in the media, in the City. Ask women in your speciality for information.

If you go to meetings you can exchange cards and ask to

meet or have lunch with someone you think might be particularly useful or who might be able to put you in touch with someone who could help.

One technique to start off an informal network is to ask close friends if they could recommend two professional people for you to talk to. This can snowball, as women managers may put you in touch with others who in turn give you other names.

As with any other social contact it helps to listen as well as talk – at least 50% of the time.

Keep the meetings brief, keep notes and, most important, repay favours in your turn and agree to meet and help other aspiring women managers with their careers. Turn from being a networker into a role model.

Advice Points
    – Consider how best to use qualifications/contacts in making a career choice.
    – Research the industry, including likely positions that would suit your talents and prospects for promotion.
    – Complete application forms truthfully.
    – Tailor your CV to the job and the industry if possible.
    – Seek out business and personal contacts willing to give you a reference. Network to find out about opportunities.
    – For management posts, stress your experience, at home, university, school, previous (including holiday) jobs.
    – Apply for training in management skills and read about the subject, before promotion if possible.
    – If you suffer discrimination in applying for jobs or promotion you can take the employer to an industrial tribunal to seek damages. However, this may not always be

the best step for your career. You could seek better opportunities elsewhere.
 – Make management aware that you want opportunities for promotion.
 – Demonstrate potential.
 – Be assertive, not aggressive.

CHAPTER 2

STARTING THE JOB

From day one you should stand up and be counted. Wallflowers are not going to do well. Don't show weakness. Be in control of yourself. (Linda – computer staff selection manager).

This chapter examines the difficulties involved in starting a new job and on taking internal promotion and strategies to handle them. We then look at how to cope with – and manage – problem people.

Preparation
The interview requires some preparation but once the contract is signed the time comes for the real homework. In your first management job, particularly, it pays to be prepared. You can work at some ideas outside the organization and, if the climate seems right, others within the firm.

The new job might require:
– Public speaking.
– Chairing meetings.
– Report writing.
– Assertiveness.

Many colleges and institutes provide evening classes or one-day Saturday courses on these topics; assertiveness courses are frequently women-only. Try them. Questa (manager in a trade association) overcame a life-time's fear of public speaking knowing that, for the new job which she desperately wanted to do, speaking at conferences was a must. She put herself on a course and despite dreadful first night nerves, coped. Within a year she was addressing conferences of 200 people without a twinge.

Less accessible are courses on managing people. Try the local tech/college but, failing that, try management textbooks and, better still, talking to people you know who are managers. (See Further Reading on page 130, particularly Drucker, Handy, Moss Kanter and O'Brien.) People like nothing better than to discuss their work. Questions like 'Who was the worst/best person you have ever managed?' will elicit detailed replies and, although you might get scare stories, you may learn from others' mistakes.

The organization may help you prepare. You could ask to meet your subordinates before the starting date. Assuming the boss interviewed you for the job you could suggest a meeting to 'clarify your main objectives'. All this gives you a chance to judge the company climate – formal/informal, conservative/liberal, calm/frenetic – and prepare for the first few days.

Making Good First Impressions
Decide, from experience gained at the interviews and other sources, how you will behave at first; i.e. try to appear calm, competent, friendly but reserved. The first few days may be bewildering but, particularly if you are the first woman in the job, you need to preserve an aura of authority and this can be done most effectively by listening calmly and not talking. Also, before you have grasped the politics of

the organization you could easily talk too much to the wrong person. A parallel is group holidays – remember getting stuck on the first night with the holiday bore, the holiday groper, the name dropper, and then spending the next two weeks avoiding him? If you admit your inexperience of managing or the speciality you are working in to all and sundry, you may find you have talked to the company sneak, the company gossip, back-stabber or whatever. At first, at least, keep mum.

New subordinates create the greatest problem. You have been selected as the most appropriate person to manage – but at the beginning they know more than you do.

Isobel (librarian in the City) described her first day as "a sod. I knew a bit about the City but there was an expectation that I knew all about kinds of information that I didn't. When you're in charge of other people it is extremely difficult to start – the people working for you know more about it than you do." Isobel has always coped by staying aloof. She cultivated good working relationships but not friends. Gradually and politely she established control over her department and respect from subordinates.

Kim's promotions in the Civil Service generally involved a movement to a different area. She had to combine the experience of being promoted with learning an entirely new job.

"I found that was always very demanding because you want to be convincing from the start and it is difficult when you don't know the field of work. I generally found that most staff were supportive and did not make my life difficult – but there were exceptions." The solution was to take her time absorbing the job before trying to introduce major changes. This is always popular with staff who generally dislike change.

In one job, she was promoted into a position from which her predecessor was being forced out against his will. "I found myself with a full two weeks' handover with him in the office. I thought that could be an extremely painful experience. Although he was gentlemanly and polite, I kept out of his way. In practice, I didn't try to start the job properly until after he had gone, otherwise I would have trodden on his feet in all respects." The drawback was that she was unable to learn from his experience but thought it a reasonable price to pay.

Naomi (advertising) came from New Zealand, so she knew little of British management style. She found it took time to understand the services provided in marketing in the UK. "I knew nothing about the geography of the UK or the people, and in marketing you desperately need that." So she asked to accompany drivers on their rounds, to get to know the people and the places with which she would have to deal, demonstrating originality as well as keenness.

Induction and Training
Sadly, many of our women managers reported no induction and no training on their appointment or promotion to management. Happily they are working constructively to prevent this happening to their successors: many have planned or started simple induction programmes which they had to invent for themselves, i.e.:
– Physical layout of the organization.
– Family tree of departments/job responsibilities.
– Organizational objectives.
– Culture of organization.
– Information on procedures (grievance, discipline, etc.).
– Sources of help: personnel, staff association, union.
– Meetings with key people involved in your job.

Many were keen, later on in the course of their jobs, to acquire training – with or without company help.

Ranee remembers well her first day as a registrar. There were two intakes of junior doctors almost on the day she started. The juniors looked to her for information on how the unit functioned. There were no consultants around and she found herself having to manage the juniors when she too was new. She had no knowledge of what the consultants expected, what their policies were for dealing with certain types of conditions and everyday mechanisms within the unit. "Very practical work issues were unknown and unclear." Ranee spent the whole day with the new intake working through these matters with them while trying to find out herself how things worked.

She learnt from that experience. Now she plans ahead for her regular intakes of junior doctors, carries out an induction programme with them and always tries to have a consultant on hand to meet them and be involved in the process.

Beth moved from accountancy into a Civil Service management job – from an aggressive commercial environment to an old-fashioned hierarchy. She not only had to cope with a complete culture shock but no induction at all. "The first day all I really got was a pass for the car park." She took matters into her own hands, phoned up everyone at her level (about a dozen people) and fixed appointments with them to find out what they did and what made the organization tick. In this way she inducted herself.

Taking the initiative yourself may be the only way. People like to talk about themselves and their work, so phoning different department heads and fixing meetings reasonably spaced out over the first few weeks could provide an excellent introduction. Find out about management courses. One of our managers persuaded her organization to pay for her to go on a diploma course in Management Studies. Another did an MBA part-time, one day a week.

An MBA lifts you in people's eyes, it says you are serious about your career – as does any form of professional qualification.

Initial Management Style

The temptation may be to go in shooting from the hip just to prove you are not the archetypal passive woman. Resist it. Listen, learn the lay of the land and plan your strategy. Learn as much as you can about key subordinates, key peers and most of all the boss before initiating changes.

The interview should give a clear idea of the organization's aims and the job's objectives – increase sales, develop new products, reduce costs, improve quality, etc. To achieve these aims you need to know the capabilities of the people, the exact limits of your authority and the degree to which your boss will support you.

Again – the first woman to do a particular management job carries a heavy responsibility. If you fail then it will be "We tried a woman in that job once – it didn't work." (If you point out that when a man mucks it up they usually pick another man, you will be met with blank incomprehension – that's different.)

Linda (computer staff selection manager) started her management job with an upfront, forthright style. She inherited basic infrastructure problems so she immediately reorganized the work, separating and mixing her subordinates. "It was management by panic," she said. She was also "vociferous" with the division's director. This made her unpopular at first "but he did listen in the end".

Caroline (personnel manager) launched in to tackle problems in her new job. "One of my staff was very good raw material, he was frustrated by the department and I knew if I led the charge he'd help. Another was one I could not do much with – he wasn't so disastrous I'd have to sack him but he was heading for retirement and I knew I could work with him. The third had to go. He wasn't surprised. He was not reskillable. He was made redundant." Her shock treatment worked without problems although with hindsight she was surprised it did not backfire. These days she is more circumspect.

Emma, moving up in her legal organization, found that what she had learnt from being in charge of a small section of the organization was not enough to prepare her for her new role. "They had a great deal of anxiety about the prospect of having a new boss and were expecting my arrival to be unpleasant."

Her approach was to ask for a list of all the staff. She thought she should meet them all as soon as possible – but exhausted herself in the process. She had to recognize firstly that the organization's problems were not of her making, next that she could not solve them over night and third that, yes, it helps to know staff – but in a large organization you need to get to know the key five or 10 subordinates first and work through them, motivating them to motivate others.

In a similar position, moving into senior management, Kim found herself with responsibility for 160 people on five different sites. "I had to recognize from the beginning that the same level of knowledge of everybody was just not feasible. You can only really manage *in absentia*, by making sure that your key representatives in each of the sites know what you stand for and how you want things to operate." With such a large span of control, Kim maintains regular contact with staff in her own office by "walking the floor".

Some of our women managers commented that they had tried too hard at the beginning to be liked by everybody or to be what people wanted them to be. This caused problems later on. Managers have to distance themselves from people and this is hard to do because we all want to be liked.

One frequently found herself 'on a pedestal' after promotion. "I was surprised early on in my promotions to find that I was not automatically included in social events. I don't think this was because I was a woman but because I frequently followed people who had operated in those jobs in an elitist way. They felt they had to treat me in the same way; it could be quite lonely." She took steps to ensure that she met people and talked to them about things other than work.

Problem Relationships
Our women managers experienced problems in establishing working relationships in many fields but these were almost exclusively with men. Some experienced resentment and hostility, and lack of support while fitting into their new management roles. Some suffered as a result of false perceptions about their jobs.

Problem groups included bosses, the new peer group and subordinates, with the greatest challenges coming from the management of subordinates who previously were colleagues and friends.

In one case, Diane, a product manager, worked in a predominantly male environment and when she was promoted her peers were jealous. "They joked about it and tried to make out it was some sort of job just to keep me happy, not in the real world." She could have rubbed their noses in it, but chose not to – "That's not a woman's way".

Her new colleagues were not so casual. They did not like her because she was assertive. "I wanted to know what they were doing and I had the courage – or some say the cheek – to say "I don't agree with that". I think they would have taken it a lot better from a man."

Another manager arrived in her most recent job as an outsider and found peers suspicious of her motives in taking the job and of what she expected to achieve from it. They thought she was using it as a short-term step to something better. She worked hard to persuade them that she genuinely wanted to work there but it took a year before they realized she had been honest in her motives.

However, the one person she did not handle well was the peer with whom she was to have the closest working relationship. "Instead of answering honestly like I did to everybody else, I thought I had to dress up some sort of longer-term vision." She did this because she thought he wanted her job and resented her presence. Her false reaction did her no good in their long-term relationship.

New subordinates also presented some difficulty to the newly promoted managers – sometimes as individuals, sometimes in a more general sense.

Newly acquired assistants may be older and more experienced and tend to be resentful. Fiona was promoted to become an editor over a number of her colleagues.

"There was a gender difference in the reaction to my

appointment. The women were very supportive and the men were ... not hostile."

Her predecessor had been most unpopular so she began in her new post by trying to ingratiate herself. She believed that if she had taken a tough line from the start "my life could have been made hell".

However, Fiona had to toughen up her approach. "I think that my peers would agree with me that when you work with colleagues you are all in the same boat. You're quite supportive of each other and you want to believe in each other. When you are the boss you have to come to come to terms with people's inadequacies. Those concerned haven't and they won't."

She noted that although you may be able to do something to improve poor performance, there may be nothing you can do about lack of ability. In a manager's job, however, you cannot gloss over this.

Tania (research manager) was also promoted over her colleagues and friends. "I found that it was quite different from what I expected. I was more experienced than the others in the department but I had been their friend. All of a sudden I was responsible for their work and I found that some of it wasn't any good. Having to tell people who were friends that they had to redo large chunks of work was horrendous – particularly when one of them argued all the time that his work was fine. The first time I tried to get him to re-write something my voice went hoarse and squeaky.

"Two of the four who worked for me accused me of changing my spots when I became a manager and, in a sense, I had. I had not realized before that, for instance, you couldn't have the whole department out for two-hour lunches with no one there to cover the phones.   It took me six months to gee up my confidence and deal with people calmly but firmly, to trust my own judgement.   Also I learned to prepare better, to work out exactly what I wanted done and how and why it needed to be done.

"I was helped by the other two in the department who adjusted to my promotion rather better than I did.   They stayed calm, kept their sense of humour and avoided taking sides between me and the other two more recalcitrant ones. They are still friends to this day.   The other two left, to my great relief, although one took his time but by the time he did go I could handle him without problems.

"I think the reasons I had problems were, firstly, no train- ing; second, no forewarning of the difficulties of managing four quite boisterous and self confident young men.   Third, I had no one to talk to about it – no support from a boss, no constructive help from the excuse of a personnel manager. Also, I had an expectation that everyone could work as I did, had the same standards and the same abilities, but two of them didn't."

Advice Points
    – Prepare as much as you can through courses, read- ing, meetings, seeking advice.
    – People expect you to know more than you do.   Be convincing but seek help.
    – Get to know the new environment, the people, the politics.   Be sensitive to others' feelings.
    – Learn from your experience – if possible imple- ment better procedures for other new joiners.
    – Try to follow an induction procedure.   Accept training courses if offered – push for them if not.
    – Take positive steps to meet people and learn what

they do, how it all fits together.

    – Changing the whole work environment on day one is probably not a good way to start even if it is in a mess. Tackle change bit by bit, so gaining acceptance.

    – Bring people together through involvement.

    – Consider the effect of your appointment on subordinates, peers and bosses and especially, on promotion, on your old colleagues who are now your subordinates.

CHAPTER 3

RELATIONS WITH SUBORDINATES

Forget your mistakes; don't worry about them for months. Don't hide in your office or you'll undermine your position and become an administrator, not a manager. (Gail – training manager).

Women in managerial jobs today are more fortunate than their predecessors. The prevailing trend is towards teamworking, coaching, listening and encouraging. All these are perceived as female characteristics and skills.

You may be lucky enough to recruit your staff yourself. More likely you will inherit a bunch of understandably wary men and women. They will, however, mostly want you to be a good boss – who wants to work for a bad one? Like an audience watching the understudy's first night they will be willing you to succeed. However, there may be elements of resentment from failed applicants and coolness at the beginning while they evaluate you. Certainly recruiting your own staff is easier; they make a commitment to you

28

when they accept the job. This chapter examines recruitment of new staff; management style; bringing out the best from individuals; building a team; dealing with older subordinates; dealing with poor performance; dealing with problem subordinates; and the differences between men and women subordinates.

Recruiting New Subordinates
As well as finding people who can demonstrate their ability to do the job, they also have to fit in with the existing team, so personality is important. Appropriate tests give an objective way of judging ability and large companies tend to use assessment centres but most managers have to depend on the interview, on whether they like the applicant and gut reaction.

It has been said that people tend to recruit in their own image and indeed our women managers tended to recruit people who cared about the job, had a sense of standards and quality very much like their own. But half an hour's talk may be misleading. It helps to check references – particularly by an informal phone call so the applicant's previous employer can be relatively honest with less fear of being held liable for damages. Listen for hints like: "I was amazed he did so well in exams," i.e. he did no work during the term. "Oh yes he's very *charming*", i.e. the charm is skin deep. Inevitably one makes mistakes. It is important to recognize these early on and to try to put them right through coaching and training for example. If this fails you may have to dismiss the recruit before unfair dismissal laws take effect (i.e. before the employee achieves two years' service).

You may decide to take on 'rookies' rather than experienced people, taking the opportunity to train and grow your own. It is anyway easier as a young manager to deal with those younger than yourself or the same age. However, there may not always be time for the 'grow from seed' approach. Sarah (estate agent) preferred to have a mixed department of men and women – "in my opinion, a fairly even split is a good one, a healthy one" – but had to make a conscious decision to recruit men in one particular job. The estate agency office was in a tough environment and she did not know of any female talent at that time. She needed results fast and did not have time to choose someone with potential and bring them on.

Most of our women managers thought that having a mixed department provided a balance of skills and strengths. One found it difficult to find suitable women sales recruits although she wanted more women in her department. As another's all-male research department expanded she decided to recruit women and some other men because she felt that a one-sex department was a bad idea. "All women – and factions develop and there's muttering behind the filing cabinets. All men – and they bore on about sports all day; everyone's language deteriorates." Another felt that in her company's "profoundly sexist environment" it raised her department's status to have some men in post. (This is backed up by research. An Equal Opportunities Commission study reports that women are paid less when working with other women and men are paid more in male-only environments.)

Having responsibility for recruitment can have a large impact on your relationship with staff. Linda (computer staff selection manager) found her male staff easier to manage than the women. The men were more straightforward, the women more sensitive and more questioning of authority. However, she had recruited the men; the women were inherited. Most, however, found female staff easier to manage.

Management Style

There are many ways of classifying managerial styles: through a matrix, through analogies or even as one writer, Gerald Mars, does by dividing managers up as, variously, vultures, hawks, wolves and donkeys. Rensis Likert defines managers as: exploitative/authoritarian (using the stick); benevolent (using the carrot); consultative (using both carrot and stick); or participative.

Another series of definitions from a management consultancy is:
Coercive – do as I tell you.
Authoritative – firm but fair.
Affiliative – people first, task second.
Democratic – participative.
Pace setting – do it myself.
Coaching – developmental.

People do not usually stick to one style only. Someone may be coaching and democratic most of the time but become authoritative when the need arises. It is not always bad to be authoritative and structured – Charles Handy writes about the 'best fit', i.e. if the work is routine and employees do not particularly want to control their own work then this is appropriate managerial behaviour. You could not, however, use close control over a creative department of designers or research scientists.

Now that organizations are less hierarchical and more likely to change in size and direction more frequently, the trend among theorists and practitioners is to look for managers who are flexible, open to new ideas, able to work in teams, likely to listen and coach. The days of the old-fashioned wielder of absolute power in a mini-prison of a department are, we hope, over. 'Empowerment' is the buzz word, meaning that all staff should be empowered to contribute. Whichever type of manager you may be, management fads for classifying styles can be useful. It never hurts to analyse your abilities under a different set of headings to find out more about yourself. Women are frequently classfied in managerial style – usually by men and often derogatorily. Men talk about 'earth mothers – always a shoulder to cry on', 'the office tart' (see Chapter 8), 'the militant feminist', 'the office pet', 'token woman', 'stroke her and she'll purr'.

Most of the above are subtle ways of sidelining women. They imply that women are there to make tea, listen to personal problems or look decorative – i.e. they are not real managers. Our women managers were aware of the risks and tried hard to be recognized for what they did and how well they did it. Many had thought about their own styles and classified their roles.

The majority who held responsibility for small teams or who had been newly promoted into their roles described themselves as 'big sisters' to their subordinates. Many had enjoyed being 'one of the boys' but found, on promotion, that this was not appropriate for their new role or that they were no longer accepted in this way. They were still able to be friendly and occasionally to socialize, but had to accept that they were the butt of office jokes and got used to being teased – as all big sisters are.

Management imposes constraints on social relationships. A good sense of camaraderie with subordinates may help working relationships – but the manager must know when the jokes have gone far enough and bring everyone back to business. How you want to be perceived may not be how you are perceived. But provided the work gets done well in a reasonable atmosphere, the manager is doing a good job. You are not in a popularity contest.

Xanthe (manager in entertainment) is nicknamed the duchess, certainly not big sister. "I have a short fuse and don't suffer fools gladly. If they louse up I may shout – but if they admit their mistakes I'll support them." She rarely goes for drinks with the boys. "I like to keep work separate from fun."

Fiona (editor) believed her style was one of mothering. She described it as "strict but supportive" and her subordinates as "bolshie adolescents. At one end of the spectrum you are very stern and tell people they have to come home at 10 pm. At the other end, you can stay up all night as long as you are responsible and I know where you are." She only exerted close control on subordinates who did not behave as she considered appropriate. She gave her staff goals and if they met them, intervention was unnecessary; if they failed to do so, she took action. One of her subordinates referred to her as "Mum" from time to time.

Vanessa (senior manager in public service) admitted she cared too much for her people. "I worry about my brood. My style varies. I can be directive or coaching. I can be open with some; others I keep at arm's length." Although caring too much for subordinates can be a problem, getting to know them can build trust and loyalty from staff and help nip any potential conflict in the bud. In one case, however, the friendly approach worked so well that one manager became a Marjorie Proops to a complete male sales team in one publishing company in which she worked. They would phone her at home and pour out their problems. "They were all super blokes," she said, "but you have to draw the line somewhere." She had to establish ground rules so that telephone calls concerned work rather than personal problems.

The personal touch may work well when you are responsible for a small number of employees. But once your span of control is too large to maintain personal contact, you need to change style to that of a leader, delegating through the ranks rather than being in touch with everything personally. However, this does not preclude a friendly management style towards all staff.

Coaching Individuals

There are many things that coaching is not. It is not simply telling people how to do things – that is teaching. It is not counselling. It is not merely telling people when they have done wrong. And it is not mentoring – mentors should not be the subordinate's immediate boss.

Coaching is the way a manager helps employees improve their work, initially showing them how to do so and monitoring them closely. Later on it should be at arm's length. The manager doing the coaching needs the ability to carry out the following.

– To hear and understand what the employee says.
– To ask open-ended questions – why should we do this? What would you do here?
– To understand the work that is to be done thoroughly.
– To recognize and praise good work frequently.
– To build trusting relationships.
– To give employees challenging opportunities.
– To provide support.

Coaching has been described (Paul Kalinaukas and Helen King, see Further Reading) as putting in skills and knowledge and pulling out commitment and expertise.

Our women managers agreed that coaching could be used to bring out the best in individual members of staff, even

34

those described as no–hopers. One style of coaching that works well is being authoritative and democratic – people know the limits within which they should work but can voice ideas freely.

Coaching means showing people how to do the work and allowing them to get on with it. It does not mean doing it for them. If a group of staff have a problem, they are usually the best people to work out how to solve it. Listening to problems that staff have is important; agreeing with them both what is wrong and the solution that is necessary for improvement. Praise when things go well but, when there are problems, the best time to criticize is just before the subordinate has a chance to perform better the second time. That way the negative energy that might be provoked by the criticism can be re-channelled into improving his or her efforts next time.

To bring out the best in individuals it is important to get to know them and to treat them with respect, in the same way you would like to be treated. If you expect honesty and trust from your boss it makes sense to provide them to your subordinates.

Giving people responsibility for their own work and putting it forward under their own name without changing it (unless absolutely necessary), so that they receive the credit for it, works to the manager's advantage, as staff become well motivated. An 'open door' policy to enable staff to communicate freely is also important.

In a good working relationship, bosses and subordinates are able to trust each other, but with one important caveat. Trust is a total thing. With subordinates your relationship needs to be defined and so trust is limited. It is sensible to take care when putting your trust in people, although if you can build trust in yourself from your subordinates, you are likely to get the best from them. Above all, people expect to be treated fairly. As children in the playground complain bitterly when the teacher is not fair, so will subordinates. If you can explain (not excuse) your actions on the basis of fairness and the needs of the work you will be well regarded.

Different Approaches

It is unlikely that you will be able to use the same management style with everybody. One of our managers found that she had to learn to treat people in different ways. She used a coaching style of management but found that she had to shout at one subordinate because otherwise he did not listen. "He shouted all the time so that was OK." He was a bluffer so she learned to call his bluff and make him check his own work without relying on her. Her strategy worked – he proved himself to be honest about admitting mistakes and was keen to put them right.

Another manager had nearly 30 people reporting to her, one third of whom were men. They were of various ages and with assorted skills. She used a supportive style of management towards her staff but found she needed to adopt a mothering style with one chap who was being bullied and with a young woman who wore provocative clothing to seek attention. She showed the man how to cope and the woman that it was unnecessary to wear such outfits simply to experience 'the cuddle factor'.

Beth (accountant) found that, in her most recent job, there was much potential among the employees in the lower grades. These lower-level jobs were predominantly held by women returning to work after maternity leave. She felt that delegating work through her managers down to these levels gave these employees more fulfilling tasks and improved their performance. The middle grades, although keen to delegate down (and so avoid shouldering the burden), were not so keen to check their subordinates' work. Beth found that she had to use 'brute force' to get her managers to accept this responsibility, consistently chasing and harrying them until they did.

She had to use a "carrot and stick" style of management although she recognized that this was not necessary for everybody. "I do have a few people working for me where it would never be appropriate to brandish a stick because they quite unreservedly give you all their best. They know I would use the stick elsewhere – they quite appreciate that and that I'm no pushover."

Building a Team
Teamworking is in vogue, particularly in large companies, but it has always been an ideal way of working. If everyone participates, everyone is involved – you put more in and you get more out. Old-fashioned but true. As with more general management styles, the theorists have devised ingenious classifications of behaviour and roles in teams. Meredith Belbin (see Further Reading) analyses eight roles, not mutually exclusive; you might have bits of two or three. They are:

Planter – creative, provides ideas   Co-ordinator
Shaper   Monitor/evaluator
Teamworker   Implementer
Completer   Specialist

Charles Margerison and Dick McCann provide a classification of nine work functions: advising, innovating, promoting, developing, organizing, producing, inspecting, maintaining and linking. These can be applied to four roles that team members adopt: explorer, adviser, organizer and controller. The above can be useful for looking at yourself or your staff in a new way.

The main points in managing teams are similar to those in coaching:
– Regular two-way communications, i.e. listening and asking questions, not just telling.
– Management by walking about, 'corridor meetings', i.e. never missing the opportunity to ask how things are going.
– Concentration on output, results.
– Monitoring, recognizing and applauding success.

Building a team requires getting everybody on to the same side. This can work well if there is a group of well motivated staff who all share a cooperative team spirit. If they do not, it is the manager's job to engineer it, to influence team members and engage their imagination and enthusiasm. However, women managers need to be cautious when using influencing skills as they are often accused of being conniving or manipulative. The way to get round this is to state objectives clearly and to make sure your body language reinforces what you are saying, using eye contact, etc. It also means making sure everyone knows the ultimate goals and the time-scale. When staff work together in teams, the manager cannot assume that all is going well. A watchful eye should be kept over the work and the relationships that develop between team members. Monitoring is a large part of management.

The current fashion for dealing with everything by setting up teams needs careful handling and preparation. The team is likely to consist of people with different levels of ability, skills and temperaments. There may be members of the team who have more experience than you. These people require a different style of management.

When a team contains a range of skill levels and includes specialists with greater experience than you have, you don't have to tell them how to do their jobs. You have to be less directional towards them, allow them the latitude to formulate work plans and just specify aims and deadlines.

Your subordinates may work well together and have a team spirit. If you, too, can be part of the team and not just 'the boss', you are likely to find this rewarding.

When Jean took up a previous job as a sales manager in a publishing company she was resented by the all-male typesetting department. A glass office was built for her – it separated her from the unionized environment of the shop-floor. She made a point of getting out of it to talk to staff members every day and take the knocks that came with it. She got to know them and identified their skills, and, as her sales grew, so their work increased – "all good for their bread and butter". They came round in the end and she felt part of the team.

Identifying concerns through personal contact is important even though this may not always seem to be the most productive use of time. The Industrial Society has for many years advised managers to 'walk the job'. One manager felt she had achieved a breakthrough when her staff on one site invited her to their Christmas lunch and made it clear that it was not just an invitation for the sake of it but that they genuinely did want her to join them. Even when accepted as part of the team, the manager's duty is firstly to the organization. Our more senior managers were aware of the staff viewpoint but, when voting at board meetings, had consciously (and at times unwillingly) to put the organization first.

Dealing with Older Subordinates
It is easier to manage subordinates who are younger than you are. They are more likely to give respect, easier to train

and mould. However, many managers will find themselves in charge of a mixed group.

Subordinates look to professionalism and experience – respect does not come through age alone. Younger women managers may have problems working with older male subordinates – either because of the men's attitudes or their own lack of confidence. If the problem is the former, remind yourself that their prejudice is their problem. Concentrate yourself and them on the task. Once you have demonstrated the ability to do the job most prejudices will abate.

Many of our women managers commented on initial difficulties in this area. Some found it more difficult dealing with older women and older men. Paula found that her male subordinates were more likely to challenge her – she believed this was a function of age, they were in their fifties.

Diane felt that managing someone 20 years older than herself did not bother her – although she recognized that he might feel depressed about being managed by a young woman. She felt that she might have to prove that she was worthy of the responsibility that she held and worthy of his trust.

Anita (consultant director) had to manage an older man early in her career. He was a retired civil servant and very clever. "It was a matter of planning, working out what was wanted and giving him a framework, something he could do well."

In another case, a younger woman manager had to manage older men recruited for special projects. They were eminent in their field but not always used to writing for publication. She found that, in the main, they coped with great courtesy and very little patronizing. She learned not to be ageist, that age does not stop people learning a new skill. "You can manage people older than yourself; it just takes a bit more effort and a bit more tact," she said.

Dealing with Poor Performance

Subordinates who undermine the boss cannot be tolerated. Most of us recognize that we cannot beat the boss; a subordinate who does not acknowledge this needs to be reminded of it. If someone is unable to accept this, there may be a need to use the disciplinary procedure or for the two of you to part company.

Poor performance may be caused by inadequate training, lack of understanding of the job or the ultimate aims of the work, bad management or even personal problems. (See Marilyn Wheeler: *Problem People at Work and How to Deal with Them* – Further Reading page 132).

The first thing for a manager to do is identify the problem and get the person concerned to accept that it exists. If this cannot be agreed it might be necessary to go further – the disciplinary procedure for instance (see Chapter 6). However, most people recognize when they are not achieving their best and want to improve. Try to eliminate personal problems first. Then try to plan with the subordinate how he or she can acquire new skills or work more quickly or develop in the direction you want. Lastly, monitor to make sure it works and give praise if it does.

Encouragement, coaching and building up self-assurance can work wonders.

Beth found that in her accountancy firm people were written off if they did not fit into the organizational style. She believed that they may have been more than adequate at doing their job but were not given a chance "because they didn't have the right accent, they didn't dress properly or they didn't have all the social graces". Often they were pushed into a corner and poor performance resulted.

Using her style of encouraging participation, she identified these employees' strong points and made sure they could develop them to their full potential. She believed that one of the best staff she had ever managed fell into this category. He had come from a difficult home life, a background that was non-compatible with the firm's partnership policy. She thought him pleasant, with intellect and a capacity for hard work. So she developed and nurtured him and, despite him being written off by the firm because of a poor start, he did extremely well in his accountancy examinations and his good work for Beth was recognized by the partners. "I brought out his full potential. It was a very satisfying experience," she said.

However, if someone cannot do the job after training, coaching, etc. there may be little that can be done. Perhaps they can be moved to another part of the organization which suits their skills better; alternatively there may be no place for them at all. "You set them objectives – they constantly fail to meet them. You set them work, tell them they are to do it and then they'll pass it to someone else. There is nothing deliberate about the poor performance if somebody is simply not up to it," said Beth.

Dealing with Problem Subordinates
"There are no bad troops, only bad officers." Charles Handy applies this to managers but, although techniques described by him and others may transform 99% of subordinates into model employees, there is always the one...

Problem subordinates experienced by our women managers included the lazy, the unmotivated and the mavericks.

Generally, our managers tackled the problems rather than passing the buck or sidestepping the issue. Sometimes they succeeded, mostly through spending time with their subordinates, explaining the problem, coaching, setting targets, etc. But not every problem subordinate was turned round.

Lazy subordinates proved to be a difficulty for some. Beth's approach was to take "an unhealthy interest" in their work. This almost always had the effect of improving performance. In one rather laid back company she worked in, jobs got passed around, with her junior managers ducking their responsibilities by handing work down to their subordinates. A new strategy was required.

"I had to get every man and his dog in my office and go through in the minutest detail what needed doing and allocate to individuals bits of it so if something did not get done I could single out the person who had not done it." This worked. Once her junior managers had some direction and guidance they became willing to take pride in their work and they did it well.

Naomi (advertising director) had two difficult male subordinates – one she described as "an old yuppie who would sell his own grandmother". He was irresponsible, precocious, but had presence. "I spent time with him, got him to realize that unless he organized himself (as well as other people) there would continue to be problems. I got past some of the arrogance. He admitted that some of the things he launched before I arrived were disasters. He became more realistic, more pragmatic. We're still friends."

The second was "tetchy". He had a very detailed mind but was hopeless at presentation and had no commercial nous. He spent his time on irrelevant things, unable to manage key relationships. Naomi talked to him about people, not data, and her strategy worked. He went into a job that involved people and he did it well.

There is a type often encountered in large organizations – the person who is highly intelligent and very perceptive but bone idle and intellectually dishonest. Such people are extremely hard to motivate and may, in the end, not be worth the effort. Nagging may work sometimes or it may prove counter-productive as Kim (civil servant) discovered. "One of my current staff recently told me he had a dream in which he was in hospital. Everything was white and then he saw me walking down the ward towards him bringing flowers. I was just beginning to feel good about this, when he said I leant over the bed and asked him if he'd finished a particular paper that I had been hassling him for. I wasn't sure how to deal with that."

Managing Men versus Women
Our women managers disagreed as to whether they had to use different management styles when managing men versus women. Some preferred to manage women; a few preferred men. However, the important thing was to get the best out of them all. As Emma said: "You have to know how to switch them on." A selection of comments are given below:

About Men	*About Women*
Men look for hidden meanings	Women are prepared to say what they think
Men need clear instructions	Women understand a female manager's short-hand
Men may try to wrong-foot you	Women can be handled on a long rein, with trust but with clear objectives

44

Men are more task orientated; less service orientated	Women are more caring
Men need more assurance	With women, what you see is what you get
Men never help each other; they never say thank you	Women are more accessible; more communicative; more open
Men do not question; they pretend to understand	Women are not worried about saving face
Men are conscientious	Women are more organized; more disciplined - with a project they will organize what and how
Men require women to assert their authority	Women are more articulate; have greater control of their feelings

The comments did point to one clear difference between managing men and women: women tend to open themselves up to a greater extent, to reveal their feelings and be willing to discuss problems. Women managers in the main found this helpful; they could be on the same wavelength as their female subordinates. On the whole, they found it easier to get into conversation with women, to discuss problems and find ways of solving them.

Nevertheless, some reported their female subordinates as being too emotional. Criticism left them mortified. Criticism of men caused problems too – although their general reaction was to become aggressive or to sulk. Some, however, found them more relaxed and able to handle criticism better than women.

If the comments seem sexist it may just be that each sex finds it easier to deal with its own kind – an excuse, perhaps, for men recruiting and promoting men. Just as we imply that male managers should discriminate less, women managers may have to make extra efforts to communicate with and deal with men.

An interesting view put forward by a few of our women managers was that their male subordinates had sometimes been over-promoted when they had inherited them. Past practices had not favoured equal opportunities and this resulted in capable women staying in lower graded jobs, with men promoted to roles beyond their abilities. This proved a challenge in the management of men versus women.

Some found that they had been able to build the closest rapport with women and had the most effective teams when women were involved. Most of the individual problems that they had encountered had been with men. However, one summary – "there are no simple comparisons between men and women" – was echoed by all our interviewees. An effective management style involves bringing out the best in people, not managing according to sexual stereotypes.

Advice Points

 – Consider recruiting raw material from which you can grow your own as well as experienced personnel.

 – Aim for a mixed team of men and women to provide balance in the working environment.

 – Don't expect to be one of the boys; once you are a manager, relationships with subordinates change, especially with ex-peers.

 – Be supportive of your staff; listen to them; coach where possible.

 – Treat your staff as you would like to be treated by your boss.

 – Use involvement to motivate employees.

— Be as fair and as consistent as possible.

— Give credit where credit is due.

— Use different management styles according to the person being managed.

— Identify latent talent and develop it.

— Become a part of the team if you can but remember you are still a manager and must put the company first.

— Do not be ageist; learn from older subordinates' wisdom; treat them with tact and respect.

— Use coaching and encouragement to improve subordinates' poor performance.

— Determine strategies to handle problem subordinates. Accept that you may not succeed with them all. You may have to compromise or take disciplinary action.

CHAPTER 4

RELATIONS WITH PEERS

Men still hate to be equalled, or worse, beaten by a woman. If they are beaten by a man, they feel that's fair and square. Being beaten by a woman, they think, is not – Cary Cooper, Professor of Psychology at the University of Manchester Institute of Science and Technology.

A supportive, friendly peer group makes the working environment enjoyable. It can also have practical advantages in terms of building a power base, networking to identify opportunities and having fun. Not all peers will be a joy to work with. Our women managers found themselves with a variety of problem people – some resenting their presence, others hostile, yet others refusing to give any support or even speak to them. This chapter examines the peer problems you are likely to encounter and strategies for building relationships within and across teams, both in-company and in other environments. First, the advantages that make these efforts worthwhile.

Advantages of a Good Peer Group
Second only to reporting to the perfect boss comes a good, supportive and effective peer group.

Competitive climates are rarely encouraged now that the emphasis is on teamworking. But the current and continuing redundancy programmes (known as 'downsizing' or even 'rightsizing') mean that colleagues may be keen to emphasize their good points and your weak ones.

Some companies used to encourage this kind of cut-throat competition between executives – it kept them concentrating on results and working long hours for no overtime. It can also lead to stress, bad judgement (after long hours) and concentration on self-promotion rather than company objectives.

If your boss encourages you and your peers to compete rather than collaborate, you will be expected to promote the same behaviour among your subordinates. All progressive management thought now acknowledges that people work better when they are coached rather than controlled, when they participate and get involved rather than back-stab to impress the boss.

So, if you find yourself in a cut-throat company, unless you are exceptionally aggressive and good with a razor, take the advice of management consultants, theorists and our cross-section of women managers – find a more progressive organization. Beating your head against a brick wall may be nice when it stops, but it causes brain damage.

If managers on the same level work towards similar goals, the nastiest parts of office politics can be avoided. Peers can provide moral support for each other to cope with a difficult boss; information, advice and understanding on dealing with problem subordinates and, if you are lucky, close friendships that last for years (authors' note).

Working to achieve this desirable state of affairs rather than working on one-upmanship policies takes time. Our women managers faced surprise and suspicion when they sought cooperation from male peers who were far more competitive. But long-term planning and persistence can work. We look at the types of problem peers may cause and how to deal with them.

Resentment

Resentment from peers can make working life difficult, even unpleasant. It can also hinder learning about how the organization functions. Caroline (personnel manager) had an automatic promotion when her manager left. She experienced much resentment from two other male managers who had technical expertise and thought they should have got the job and from another man, below them, who saw her as blocking his career path. "They accused me of making up to the CEO – not sleeping with him but getting on his good side. It was like being in the playground with a load of bullies." She tried to talk to them, meeting outside the organization over a drink to discuss "the problem" coolly. Individually and as a group they remained unrepentant. She was a woman and not good enough for the job, they thought. Nothing would change their minds. She ignored them and has since left them behind on the promotion ladder.

Olivia's (engineer) relationships with her all-male peers were generally very good. She had to work with people in her own team and interact with others in associated teams. All worked together to ensure design, development, testing, etc. went smoothly. However, she found that one man in another division refused to work with her. She offered to discuss her work with him but he would not respond, saying he would only discuss it with her boss. She let him and watched with amusement as correspondence went back and forth between them while she remained "out of the loop". Ultimately this man would do himself more damage than he could do her. Her own boss would become irritated with the extra work and her peer would eventually be seen as a prejudiced pedant.

In cases of extreme prejudices like the two above, once you have tried to be reasonable and you continue to be treated unreasonably, the only solution is to distance yourself, making it clear to any other interested parties (i.e. your boss and other managers) that you continue to leave the door open for your recalcitrant peer to talk to you should he see the error of his ways. A little patronizing does not do any harm – claim the high ground. A supportive boss may help by intervening. More often your own hard work and competence should help you win acceptance from most of your peers, most of the time, provided that you do not gossip about the problem or try back-stabbing – calm martyrdom looks better on the personnel file.

Lack of Support
A woman manager in an all-male environment may simply not fit in to start with – especially if the group has a particularly macho culture. Beth (accountant) found that the other managers accepted her as a manager but, although they socialized, she was left out. "Socializing revolved around football, rugger and going to the pub. I have very little interest in this and there was little point trying to pretend. I made it clear that I wasn't interested in sporty events – it wasn't my style." Because of this she was also excluded from other social events.

The real problem was that she had no links with her peers and their manager. So, to find out what to do in her new job, she had to seek advice from previous colleagues. This was unsatisfactory because the different sections of the organization had different practices. "I had nobody to help me with the ropes whereas I had a colleague in the same group who was male, sporty and promoted at the same time who had hours of help lavished on him. I thought it was grossly unfair."

It seems that Beth's boss should at least have taken the responsibility to coach her in her new job. As he failed she had to work around him. But if you are stuck in an all-male peer group it does not hurt to compromize a little – not all sports are boring to all women. If you listen to rugger stories for a while they might be prepared to listen to what interests you later. Once you are inside a group it is a great deal easier to influence it. In the US, women managers say, only half joking, that learning golf is compulsory because that is where the real deals get done – on the green and in the clubhouse. That kind of culture may be discriminatory but you cannot change it overnight.

Power Struggles

Peer politics are part of everyday life with jockeying for position and professional competition a common phenomenon. Power struggles are another matter and can become unpleasant if not dangerous, especially to the unwary.

Sarah (estate agent) joined a new company, working with a group of men. She put forward new ideas and began to get noticed by the MD. This put her out of favour with one of her colleagues and heavily in favour with another. She had no idea that a power battle was taking place between them. She built up a strong bond with one man but he left, unable to take the political infighting. This left Sarah with no support, indeed with a very hostile colleague. At the same time, two new male staff members had joined and they formed a bond, with one backing the other. When she was promoted above all of them, her male colleagues' relationship with the MD deteriorated and although she was congratulated by her ex-peers ("all sweetness and light to my face"), they both resigned. The hostile one left too and she knew his departure was because of her. She felt this was a terrible loss of colleagues, blamed herself and offered to resign her directorship, which was refused.

"I think it would be naive of me to say that I was just the innocent casualty. I am young, successful, reasonably intelligent and a woman – and all those are sins so you are unacceptable, you are a freak."

This case seemed intractable. The best solution for coping with continuing hostility, power politics and indifference from on high might be to find a better-run company.

Building Relationships
Strategies to build relationships among colleagues and to gain their acceptance varied from drip-feeding help, support and sympathy and so building trust and loyalty, to public showdowns and confrontation. Whichever approach is taken, it may not be possible to build a good relationship with all your peers either in your own work group or across teams/functions. Taking steps to gain the support of a critical few is necessary to achieve some harmony at work.

Hard work and persistence pay off in building relationships with colleagues. Two of our interviewees made a conscious decision to build a support group and both, over time, succeeded.

Beth (accountant) believed in the value of hard work. "I always thought that if you could prove that you could do the job better than a man, then you were accepted." She used this as part of her strategy to get female colleagues on board.

"There was always a minority of women, so it seemed to me that if I got on with them they would come alongside me." So she built her power base, as she described it, on her own terms. Her reputation grew. She was perceived by the men as having a huge amount of technical expertise and they began to come to her for advice. In the macho culture they did not feel able to ask their male colleagues for help. "They would slink into my office and say 'I've got a problem, what should I do?' and I would help them. They would come to me because I wouldn't tell them they were stupid."

Her support base grew as colleagues came to trust her, knowing she would not give them an answer "just to fob them off", guess or show off an ego. She was genuinely interested in getting an answer right and quietly helping them with their work.

But, in another earlier job, Beth found that the only course of action open to her was a public showdown. A male peer criticized her specialist knowledge in a nasty memo circulated around the building by e-mail. Because their disagreement was so public she decided her best course of action was to fight her corner. She replied incisively and this told her peers firmly that she was 'her own man'. She found that colleagues came to her office to give her moral support as they felt his treatment of her had been wrong.

Later on, another male manager publicly criticized Beth's department. She had a shouting match with him. She was not proud of this but felt that she had to set the record straight against his false accusations. Other parts of the organization then realized that her department was a force to be reckoned with. When all else fails it may be necessary to fight back.

Fiona (editor) stressed the importance of building trust in her peer group. "It sounds terribly corny but if you are straight and reliable and you care about other people, then they will probably respond."

Fiona's small group of supportive male peers took some while to build their relationship but she felt it was worth a great deal. She does not describe them as friends but people who have been in the organization for a similar amount of time, who all had the traumas of the selection process – being promoted from within and therefore having worked at the same level before. "We all have one mind on an awful lot of things." Together they have forged a strong power base, support each other in public and have a stronger influence than they could have done individually over their boss.

Ranee (doctor) had to make more effort to get on well with other teams as well as her peers – patient care depended upon it. "There are whole groups of other people – nursing staff, paramedical staff, clerical staff – whom you have to establish relationships with that you've never known before, and that can take a very long time. I try to establish a relationship on an equal footing rather than being senior or an expert. I make it very clear that I see everybody having an important role, that all our roles are different and that we all have something to contribute. Together we can manage a patient or the family effectively."

To build bridges to other teams she needed the support of

her own peer group. "We are all in the same boat and there's almost a sense of solidarity about what we are doing versus the management, the consultant staff and sometimes the nursing staff. They are not quite the enemy but we are all struggling to keep those working relationships going. It's hard and therefore we cannot afford to snipe at each other. I'm lucky – most of my colleagues at my level are very amenable and we can talk through all that we are feeling."

She felt accepted when she found herself on the grapevine. She started to hear about how she was regarded and this made her feel a part of the unit. When she had first started she had felt quite outside this camaraderie.

The self-employed and those running their own business can benefit from building relationships with peers outside. Building trust among potential clients can be a precursor to doing business. Good relationships with clients and/or potential clients can also result in new business leads. Some – with whom you establish especially good relations – may even take steps to promote your work among their contacts.

A period of trust building in developing a business relationship requires patience and should not be viewed as a waste of time. If the client is the sort of person who is interested in developing a relationship with you, you have more chance of getting the business than with the type who says "where's your brochure? I'll read it later, goodbye."

Networking
Building relationships with peers in industry helps to make new contacts. When clients are genuinely interested in your business, they want to help you to do it. They are either interested in you personally or in the business, it doesn't

56

really matter which; the end result is the same.

Developing good contacts in your industry group and/or within your organization keeps you abreast of new opportunities. Several of our women managers said that they had heard about job opportunities through the grapevine – with successful results.

Networking should be used well – you need to make the right kind of networks, not necessarily women only. One manager said: "I've learnt to use networks, to make sure I repay favours." She also used other avenues to further her career such as non-executive directorships. It all helps in the growth of expertise.

Advice Points
If you have problem peers whom you would like on your side:
    – Try to understand why they are unwilling to build a relationship with you.
    – Decide what you want to achieve: to diffuse resentment, to build support, to seek friendship?
    – Consider whether you can seek help/support from your boss or other peers.
    – Try a strategy of helping/supporting your problem peer, avoiding confrontation unless necessary.
    – Show empathy, respect and loyalty.
    – Stay loyal; do not gossip about your peers. Build up your own reputation and peer group.

CHAPTER 5

RELATIONS WITH THE BOSS

The most important thing about your job is.....? (Answer below)
– John Garnett, former Director, Industrial Society.

The director of a training institution used to like conducting induction sessions for new staff himself. He would ask the 12 or 15 people individually why they had left their previous job and note the answer. He would ask what was the best thing about their old job. On a flip chart he would list the most common replies.

People left because:
– They had no responsibility.
– They were bored with the work.
– They wanted to move up and were stuck.

And many more. Slowly he would draw their attention to the common denominator – in the bad points about their job and the good. Then he would announce, with fervour and

58

conviction and in capital letters:

THE MOST IMPORTANT THING ABOUT YOUR JOB IS YOUR BOSS

And he was right.

As our previous chapters have shown people can learn to cope with obstreperous peers, lazy subordinates, etc. But an inadequate or overbearing boss makes everyone's working life a misery, whereas a good one makes the day a challenge. Ask your friends why they left jobs; ask yourself. Almost always the answer is the foibles of the boss, whether a bully or a wimp incapable of supporting staff. Even if the answer is money, who determines pay usually? The boss. And pay itself is recognition – motivation from the person to whom you report. Just as you cannot beat the bad boss, you remember the good ones forever. This chapter deals with the good, the bad and the mad and how to cope. But it is worth asking yourself: which category of boss are you?

We show how to survive and deal with – even come out ahead of – the bad experiences and how to learn lessons in how not to behave, to be one of the good bosses of the future.

What Makes a Good Boss?
Many books deal with this. Some how-to books even show you how to make your boss better. (See Further Reading on page 130) We are all agreed on the qualities of a good boss. Such people:
– Recognize professional women's abilities.
– Develop subordinates.
– Delegate power and control.
– Take action and do not let things drift.
– Communicate openly.

– Are open-minded, honest and fair in approach.
– Spend time with people.

Many commented that the best bosses did not feel threatened by them. Paula (finance controller) said that one of her bosses was nearing retirement and she thought that this might have been why he was so helpful and supportive.

"He developed me a lot, gave me opportunities. He would take me to meetings to which I had not been invited. I'd write papers and he would *say* I'd written them. He'd help with the detail of the work." The fact that she points to his recognition of her work publicly shows how many others do not behave like this, accepting praise for work done by subordinates.

Others felt that their bosses' family circumstances influenced their thinking towards women. Men who have helped bring up families are often more considerate of those with family responsibilities, and men with expectations for their daughters understand aspiring women mangers.

On management style, bosses who exercized too much control over their staff may have run effective departments but this did not result in motivated individuals. A very tight ship may mean that there isn't much scope for innovation.

Bosses who allowed some autonomy were appreciated more. This enabled our women managers to control their own work and gave them the opportunity to learn from their mistakes.

Bosses who delegated responsibility, combined with authority, to their managers were admired both for the trust that they had placed in their subordinates and for the development opportunities that this action presented. Those who dealt with problems quickly were also appreciated. Using skills like persuasiveness rather than manipulation, combined with firmness, was admired too. Successful bosses got results this way.

Another quality, much admired and used with great skill by some bosses, was open-mindedness. Combined with honesty and fairness, this brought results from subordinates and they were role models to their women managers.

Busy bosses can often be too preoccupied with their own concerns to take time to discuss those of their subordinates. Our women managers recognized this and many did not expect them to do so. However, those who did spend time with their staff were highly appreciated.

Putting it into Practice
The qualities of a good boss were recognized and taken into our women managers' own management style. Sarah said about her current boss: "I think we have a very special relationship in that we are so honest with each other and I encourage this with my managers. If they are hacked off with me, they tell me. I tell him how I feel; it works both ways." Several found that coaching and developing their charges was both personally as well as professionally rewarding (see Chapter 3, page 34).

What Makes a Bad Boss?
Problem bosses are those who:
– Refuse to recognize women's abilities.
– Discriminate/harass women at work.
– Have a macho attitude towards staff.
– Lie and back-stab for their own ends.
– Manipulate and operate divide-and-rule strategies.
– Undermine their subordinates.

– Are inefficient and incompetent either in management skills and/or technical expertise
– Make you wonder whether they are mad or you are.

The best way of dealing with bad bosses is to avoid them altogether. Naomi (advertising director) said: "At the first interview I thought my potential boss would be an intellectual inspiration but we didn't agree on anything. But I believed in the company so I thought I could discount him. It was horrendous. He provided no nurturing, coaching and everyone was battered by character assassination. I had ignored all the signals at the interview." People in the department were leaving in droves. Just as she was about to go herself, driven out after six months, he left.

'Male Only' Culture and Discrimination
Dealing with a 'male only' culture at the top of an organization was a common problem. For some, this simply amounted to a lack of understanding of women managers.

Some male managers still have no understanding of women's right to decide their own destinies – they are to be protected and looked after; they are not real people. If they have kids they should be at home. To teach men like that how to behave with women (i.e. the same way they do with men) is often like pulling teeth.

However, male cultures can result in lost opportunities, discrimination and harassment for some women (see Chapters 6 and 8). Managers who are patronizing or who fail to take women seriously can alienate female subordinates and end up losing their respect.

Those who had experienced direct discrimination felt that it often resulted from the male boss's initial assumption that a woman would not be up to the job. Women may find that they have to prove their worth, whereas a man's competence may be taken for granted.

Solving this problem is not easy. Women managers can work hard to prove themselves and overcome their bosses' prejudices. But the answer may lie in looking for a better climate of equal opportunities elsewhere (see Chapter 6). For some women, harassment by their boss made the working relationship impossible (see Chapter 8).

Macho Attitudes
"My direct boss swears every other word, shows no respect, needs someone to shout at. He's inarticulate and therefore needs to get rid of his frustrations."

Loud, aggressive, macho behaviour is intimidating – both to men and women. It certainly does not bring out the best in subordinates. It frequently reflects an inability to do the job. Generally, our women managers tended to work around such characters, avoiding them when possible.

Dealing with Hostility and Back-stabbing
The macho boss went further than just shouting and swearing, for some of our managers. And when his actions affected their professional reputations, they themselves took action.

Diane (product manager) found herself reporting to someone who had been brought in to do a specific job which he was not qualified to do. "Nobody had bothered to check this out in advance. He was a classic salesman, a cartoon character, somebody who had a dozen cigarettes coming out of his mouth all over the place, hugely fat and shouting all the time. I thought (a) why is he on this planet? (b) why is he in this office? and (c) why am I reporting to him?"

He decided that she was a threat to him, made up a "whole catalogue of lies" about her and put them in writing. Diane immediately responded. She took action and refuted every lie but felt that the incident dogged her for a year. She was perceived as a troublemaker and although, eventually, the senior management realized her boss was lying (and he resigned), she felt sure it was a blot on her CV.

Dealing with Manipulative Bosses

To be undermined is humiliating. It can damage your credibility among staff, clients, etc. Often bosses who undermine their managers do so to retain their own power or to save face, although sometimes it is a personal attack. Either way, action can be taken to resolve it.

Bosses who divide and rule are often skilful political operators who use people for their own ends. This strategy can be used to keep power but it does not provide leadership.

The way to handle bosses who divide and rule is forge alliances with your peers. Diane's cartoon character boss succeeded with his divide-and-rule strategy for six months. Her colleagues were all male and there was considerable bonding between them. She was cut off. But as she made her way into their group and they reported together, so his divide-and-rule technique failed.

Commenting on her boss, Fiona (editor) said: "If you are insecure you have to turn to him the whole time for validation and if you don't get it, you are always insecure and you don't ever have enough security to challenge him." Her situation reinforces the advantages of forming strategic alliances. In her organization she and a number of peers report directly to one manager. "He had all the power and we, as a group, had very little because we were divided." She admitted that she can only get what she wants through this person. It would not make sense to attempt political manoeuvres by going through the level above.

"Each one of my peers was totally isolated. People did not cooperate with each other at all. I have forged two alliances and now there is this threesome who are very powerful, and the people in it are guaranteed always to support each other in public. Our boss is an accessible person but what has made the difference is the power we have built up. He pays more attention to us than other people because we are a group. Nobody else can be guaranteed any support from anywhere, whereas we can."

Still, individually, she has problems with him. "Probably the most significant problem for me is being undermined. To retain his power my boss undermines me along with all my peers – it's not personal. I have told him this over and over again in a constructive way. I have got it through to him that I understand what's happening, I'm not very happy about it and I don't think it's a reasonable way to behave – I think he has modified his behaviour to some extent." If your boss knows that you will respond instantly to sneaky behaviour you may be able to teach him better manners.

Jean, (chief executive) in a previous job, had spent a weekend preparing accounts and projections for a meeting with her boss and the company's accountants. Her work was dismissed by her boss in the meeting with the words "I think we ought to have these looked at by someone who knows what they're doing." The accountant defended her work in public. After the meeting Jean warned her boss never to underestimate her again. She thought he had wanted to save face, not having done the work himself.

Dealing with Inefficiency and Incompetence
Inefficient and incompetent bosses may have technical but
no managerial skills or vice versa. They may have neither.
Reporting to such individuals may be annoying and frustrating – especially if it hinders the work of the team – but
nevertheless they usually cannot be totally ignored. They
may even have some qualities which are useful.

Tactics for dealing with inefficient management include:
    – "I think you manoeuvre round them, or try to get
some direct input into what they're doing, so that you have
an opportunity to steer them."

    – "I think you have to try and learn where they are
inefficient and try and get around it by doing what they
should have been doing yourself."

    – "I tend to go to these people and say, 'look I really
do feel ...' I tend to use my interpersonal skills to get my
point of view over."

Beth (accountant) had another boss who was acute political-
ly but there was an intellectual chasm between them. He
was over-promoted. She thought him kind and quite helpful as he informed her of the office politics but was annoyed
by his insistence on her explaining the technical nature of
her work which he did not understand. She felt this was a
complete waste of everybody's time. Her solution was to
avoid him – and it worked. "I consciously adopted the
strategy of never telling him anything. I would never seek
an audience with him. Gradually he began to spend time
on other things which gave him more cause for concern."

Questa (manager in a trade association) had a boss who
either refused to delegate, keeping all the work to himself
until the overload resulted in missed deadlines or "abdicat-

ed all responsibility and concern for the bits he wasn't interested in," again leaving work undone. She found that she had to badger him constantly to find out what needed doing and nag to get him to do work for which he was responsible. "It was a highly unsatisfactory way of working and put me under a great deal of stress but I had to make him delegate work to me. However, I think he appreciated my keenness to get things off his desk and on to mine. It raised my standing as an efficient and motivated employee."

Nepotism
Where nepotism affects working relationships, it may be impossible to do anything about it.

Una (retail manager) worked for the son of the firm's managing director. Brought in because he had failed in another profession he was no better in retail – particularly with staff. Despite not knowing the business and not knowing how to manage, everyone knew he was there for life. "His father refused to recognize his inadequacies and now he runs the firm." She left for a job where she was rewarded on merit.

Managing Upward
Managing upward may be particularly important when you have an inefficient or incompetent boss. But it is also a useful method of communicating the needs of your department and in getting your own way. Various tactics have been used by our women managers.

Paula (finance controller) said: "I use being a woman. The MD likes to be flattered by a woman – he likes flirting." This may get you your own way – but can harm your reputation. "She flutters her eyelids and gets on with him" was a criticism Paula had to face.

Anita's (senior consultant) approach makes good use of interpersonal skills. "To manage people, particularly men, upward, you have to use PR, influencing and communicating skills. Be very clear what you want, when you want it, when you are going to discuss progress."

However, communicating something may not be enough. To change the habits of a lifetime you may have to remind continuously and reinforce each message. Forging alliances also serves you well in handling difficult managers.

The Bad and the Mad
Xanthe (manager in the entertainment industry) was already a fully competent middle manager, representing the firm at conferences, etc., when a new director arrived. He refused to allow any of the department to outside events – he went himself. He tried to keep everyone down.

"He was terrified of women, despite being a womanizer. He couldn't face the idea of women taking over from him. We put up with it for years. We were all victims of his power. I refused to be pushed out, I sat him out."

She and colleagues worked round him, despite him. He pushed one person out, failed with another when the union intervened. "I could have stabbed him in the back with other members of senior management whom I knew well but I couldn't behave like that. But when he left, my subsequent boss changed my life."

No matter what techniques are used to deal with problem bosses, there may be no solution other than to preserve your sanity by leaving. As Linda (computer staff selection manager) said: "In my previous job, my boss was a nightmare, Greek, borderline insane but charismatic. He'd fire people and invite them back the next day. He was very patronizing towards women. I left."

Advice Points
- If your boss lacks confidence in your abilities, become involved/break down the "male only" barrier, challenge your boss to delegate. Prove your worth.
- If you suffer discrimination/harassment from your boss, take action (see Chapters 6 and 8).
- Try to ignore macho behaviour.
- Act if faced with hostility; keep records; put forward your views; seek help from senior management.
- Form alliances with your peers; prevent divide-and-rule strategies from working; develop your own power base.
- If you are undermined explain to your boss why this is a problem, how it damages both your credibility and the work of the company.
- Handle inefficient management with care – select the best option before taking action (work around them, guide them or confront them). Remember your career may rest with them.
- Manage upward to get what you want and to help your team.
- Learn from your boss's bad points as well as the good ones and so develop your own management style. Remember how you like to be treated: while analysing your boss, your staff are doing the same to you.

CHAPTER 6

DEALING WITH DISCRIMINATION

Suffer women once to arrive at an equality with you, and they will from that moment become your superiors – Cato the Censor.

A senior manager at the BBC, when she received a double promotion over men who had previously been her bosses, was horrified by the games played at meetings. She said she had four options:

1. Play the games and object;
2. Play the games and don't object;
3. Don't play the games and object;
4. Don't play the games and don't object.

She said she took the first because "life has to go on, so you have to play the games but you can try to change the rules by objecting". This chapter examines discrimination and suggests how to tackle it and when to step back. The law says that employers should not discriminate – on pay, benefits, training, promotion, etc. The facts say that they continue to do so. Women's earnings were on average 79% of men's in 1993, up from 71% in 1975. Fewer women between 16 and 24 years of age receive job-related training (346,000 females, 403,000 males in 1993).

At least the situation is improving, you might think. But although women's pay is creeping closer to men's, and women in the armed forces can sue their ex-employers for firing them because of pregnancy (the Ministry of Defence has paid out £30 million so far), women cannot get truly equal pay unless they get appointed or promoted to the higher echelons of work.

Our women managers have found – and the national statistics prove it – that those (usually men) who appoint managers, teachers, lawyers and doctors to the top jobs usually choose men.
  – Half the law graduates each year are female but women make up only 5–6% of QCs and 8% of judges.
  – A quarter of teachers are female; only 5% of professors are women.
  – Half medical graduates are female: but only 17% of medical consultants and 4% of general surgeons are women.

The number of women managers is actually falling slightly, according to the Institute of Management (survey in Autumn 1994). Women make up only 3% of directors and there are depressingly few female chief executives. The Equal Opportunities Commission (EOC) estimates that 4,000 pregnant women are sacked every year despite new laws to prevent this.

So how can women managers counteract the attitudes that lead to and perpetuate discrimination? Below we give the definitions of discrimination and our interviewees' experiences.

What is Discrimination?

It is against the law for employers to treat anyone, on the grounds of sex, less favourably than a person of the opposite sex would be treated in the same circumstances. It is also unlawful to discriminate against people who are married. This is based on the Sex Discrimination Act 1975, amended in 1986. It, and the Equal Pay Act 1970 as amended, cover:

> – Pay: like work; work rated as equivalent; work of equal value.
> – Benefits.
> – Appointment to a job (and advertising for it).
> – Training.
> – Promotion.
> – Dismissal.

Direct discrimination means treating a woman less favourably than a man because she is a woman: e.g. male and female separate pay scales for the same or similar work; male managers receiving larger company cars than female managers; making women redundant first. The European Court of Justice ruled in 1994 that any employer who sacks a woman for being pregnant will automatically be guilty of discrimination.

Indirect discrimination means that conditions which are applied to all favour one sex more than the other and cannot be justified. For instance, if an employer insisted on height or weight limits before employing clerks, more women than men would be unlikely to comply.

However, an employer may discriminate if there is a genuine occupational qualification, e.g. actors.

Action
There are two routes that can be taken to gain redress from discrimination: an industrial tribunal or a county court (sheriff's court in Scotland). The more usual used to be the tribunal but, perhaps because there used to be restrictions on the amount of money complainants could win from a tribunal, many more people were suing for damages in the county court. Now the ceiling on damages at tribunals has been removed.

Complaints under the Sex Discrimination Act to a tribunal have to be presented no later than three months less one day from the time when the act complained about was committed. Exceptions may be made to this if there are special reasons for delay. With the county court, proceedings must be started within six months from when the discrimination took place. Under the Equal Pay Act, also, any complaint must be made within six months of leaving the job.

The EOC recommends obtaining a Sex Discrimination Act questionnaire form to send to the person whose conduct creates the problem. This could later be used in evidence in either tribunal or court. It can be obtained from Jobcentres, unemployment benefit offices or the EOC (see page 104 for addresses and phone numbers). The EOC can also provide guides to the law and advice. Most people, however, would prefer to deal with discrimination by reducing, circumventing or preventing it.

Discrimination at the Interview
It used to start with the job advert. When the law made it mostly illegal to advertize for one sex only, some male advertisers used to stipulate 'hairy chests' or 'prepared to

73

discuss sport all day' in what they perceived as a witty way of discouraging female applicants.

Now the process is delayed to the job interview where, particularly, married women among our interviewees were asked what plans they had to have children. This is discriminatory because in similar circumstances most men would not be asked that question.

Tania (research manager), although single, has frequently been asked about plans for marriage or children. "Twenty years ago it was standard. Now employers tend to skirt round it, pretend they are not really asking, but...? They know it's discriminatory but they still ask women when they would not ask men. I always told them straight out. It's hardly worth accusing a potential employer of discrimination, you simply wouldn't get the job." If they were overtly sexist at the interview, she felt she would not take the job.

Questa (manager in a trade association) found at her interview that the personnel manager kept peering at her lap (where she had placed her hands). "He peered, leaned forward, squinted, shuffled in his seat. He was trying to identify something. As I moved my hands, his eyes followed them. It dawned on me he was trying to see if I wore a wedding or engagement ring." So she thrust her left hand under his nose to make the point. "He told me he wasn't allowed to ask me if I was married or planning marriage so I put him out of his misery. He was very sheepish about it but it was blatantly discriminatory. I was single then and got the job."

At an interview to become manager of a branch (she already worked for the firm), Sarah encountered one highly sexist director of the company. She was the sole woman of nine candidates. "He was close to retirement. He was patronizing, rude and asked me very personal questions. He summed up by saying 'Yes, well you are very impressive and you'll make a wonderful Sunday lady (part-timer) when you've had children', and put my application in the bin." Sarah cooled the steam coming out of her ears and reported the incident to her own group director, who had supported her application. "He was furious." The other manager who had helped interview her and had seen her anger apologized and begged her not to take further action. She decided it was in her best interest not to, but moved on soon after.

Promotion Discrimination

Some excuses for discrimination by those inflicting it can be bizarre. In one case a woman manager was given her boss's job when he retired but not the directorship that he had. She discovered the reason was that the directors (all male) used to go for golfing weekends "and we thought you'd be uncomfortable doing that".

Margaret (biochemist) has seen changes to promotion patterns, in and out of the public sector. Before the unit she worked in was privatized "it was patriarchal, all the managers were men, nearly all the women were technicians". It changed rapidly, particularly after privatization. "It looked like positive discrimination but I don't think it was a conscious policy."

Despite this she felt it was still harder for women to be promoted than men. "It may have been coincidence but, when there were both sexes at lower levels the men were promoted first. When there were no longer any experienced men at that level, they started promoting women."

Emma has found little discrimination in her area of the law

but she works in London and has no children. "Within my organization women account for 45% of senior posts. Elsewhere in the country the percentage has been as low as 2%." She also said that women she knew in senior positions were mostly childless.

Ranee confirmed the statistics on doctors. "In my own speciality (paediatrics) I think it is better weighted than in, say, surgery. I know of surgeons who have said 'well, a woman couldn't do this job'. But I haven't experienced it personally."

Pay and Benefits

It is hard to take action over discrimination at the level of recruitment and promotion – and it might hurt your career if you handled things badly. However, specific discriminatory treatment on pay and benefits can be dealt with. One of our woman managers threatened a previous employer with a tribunal unless they gave her a car – all the male managers in the company had cars. "I threatened them with a 'work of equal value' case. I got my car."

Beth was given a worse car than contemporaries on her return from maternity leave but did not complain. "It functioned adequately and I didn't think making a fuss was worth the aggravation." What concerned her more were suspicions that she was paid less because she was a woman. Because pay scales were kept secret she could not prove it. "Many male colleagues were not prepared to discuss it and I was only prepared to go so far in discussing it with them." Perhaps if she had been more open she could have discovered the facts and taken action.

Early in her career Sarah met blatant discrimination and voted with her feet. She noticed that men in the estate agency where she worked were getting promoted and women were not. "I said to the personnel manager, 'I can't help noticing that I've been around a little while longer than some of these people and they are being promoted over my head – am I doing something wrong?'" He told her that she could run the sales team in a new branch. "But you're not going to have the title manager or go to managers' meetings because we don't have women managers." He told her that she had a smaller car than her colleagues because she was a girl and needed something that was easy to handle.

She made her views clear: she would not take the job under discriminatory terms and left for a better job. In fact she was head hunted partly for her qualities of stirring up all-male environments which she did successfully, despite catching her young boss "doing something he shouldn't with the Sunday lady". He discriminated against her by giving her the worst areas to work in. She coped by making more money out of them than he did out of better areas, so the directors responded by giving her management training and a promotion.

Sometimes it pays to be bolshie, as Sarah found, or to work hard and prove the discrimination wrong. But with entrenched attitudes, voting with your feet might be better for your career than taking the boss to court. One of our managers discovered that a male colleague got a rise because he had started a family; a female colleague with a dependent mother did not. All her male colleagues received free newspapers for a year before her boss "remembered" to tell her she could have them too. "Finally one male colleague pulled ahead of me in pay. I confronted my boss, pointed out that my department was making more money than the previous year while my colleague's was making less. 'That', my boss said, 'was why he got the rise'. He felt sorry for him. It was the last straw – I left soon afterwards."

Parent Prejudice

Many managers, women as well as men, carry their personal prejudices with them to work. It is apparently quite permissible for fathers to work all hours but not mothers. Both Diane (product manager) and Beth (accountant) faced discrimination on this. Diane's boss told her even before she gave birth, that having a baby would stand in the way of any chance of promotion.

Despite the fact that this was completely against the firm's personnel policies, Diane did not use the grievance procedure. She chose instead to prove the man wrong. After maternity leave she went back to work full time. "I was quite hard-nosed about it, I said 'right, if you are going to be such a bastard I'll work full time, but I reserve the right to go part time after my second child'." Which she has done.

Beth took a harder line. When she returned from maternity leave her boss suggested she should go back home and look after her children. She made an official complaint through the grievance procedure. "I got a very positive reaction – they couldn't really do anything else." She received an apology from one of the most senior managers. She handled the affair tactfully, concerned that she might be labelled a troublemaker. She told no one else in the organization about the remarks or the results of the grievance procedure.

Beth remained working for the same man for some time. It was awkward and she would have preferred to have been moved but she was civil to him and eventually he realized and acknowledged her competence. "I have found again and again that men assume that you won't be up to it." This incident led to her questioning her future with the firm.

Although senior management had been appropriately apologetic she noted the tiny minority of women partners and two years later chose to move to an organization which she could see promoted and valued women. In her current job "women at higher grades do have as good a chance as their male peers".

Girls Can't Play – It's a Boys' Game
Finally in the discrimination stakes is the notion that women really are not cut out to be managers, should not tell men what to do and are unfeminine to want to do so. The more mature of our interviewees had recognized this as standard 20 years ago (although they had fought it then, as now) and felt that attitudes had changed. But it is still commonplace for women to be called girls and generally patronized by some men. Two or three of our women managers pointed out that it was generally the insecure man who acted this way – either unhappy about his job or perhaps his sexuality.

Wanda (lawyer/accountant) found colleagues at a meeting apologizing for saying "damn" in front of 'ladies'. She waited her chance, stood up and said in dulcet tones "Gentlemen, with respect you are talking a load of f***ing s***." Crude – but it worked. If you do not feel up to such shock treatment, talk to them adult to adult – when someone treats you like a child treat them like an adult not a parent. If told "girls can't do mechanical things" the best response is not "they can so" but "you're holding that widget responsifier upside down."

One of our managers pointed out to her boss that there were no women role models in the company. He said there was no need – women weren't real managers. It seems that deep down some men find the idea of women with power disturbing.

79

Some cope by patronizing. Our consultant director Anita worked for one client where the board of directors obviously were not expecting a woman to teach them how to improve their business. "They did not understand that I had international experience in my field. All they could see was this plump mum. They tried to undermine me, really went for the jugular." She brought in two extra staff to run workshops and happened to use two women because they were the best for that particular job. "I should have taken along some male drongo to feed back to them that 'actually she has a world-class reputation'." She survived and kept the business but felt even when she had finished the job that they could not acknowledge that women have intellectual ability.

Reverse Discrimination
Fiona (editor) has seen another sort of discrimination at work: women showing prejudice against men. "There's a sisterhood in our organization which I find extremely oppressive because there's a lot of hostility to men – all the women have to stick together. They are completely unscrupulous as far as I am concerned; they're perfectly happy to discriminate against the men in their attitude but they would be absolutely outraged if the men did the same thing back again. They expect anyone else who is female to want to be an enthusiastic part of all this and I find it totally obnoxious." At one point the sisterhood expected her to back a woman against a man on the basis of sex rather than abilities and she refused. She was astonished to find even some men had expected her to side with the women.

Positive Action
Two of our women managers were beneficiaries of positive action. Paula (finance controller) found herself working for a new MD. Within three weeks she was promoted. "He is

married with two daughters and he treats me like one of his daughters. He worries about my welfare and he wants to get the first woman on the board." She was concerned, however, about whether her boss was taking positive action to fulfil his own ambition and whether she was good enough for the next step up – directorship.

Kim's first management job in the Civil Service came through patronage. Her boss wanted her for the job and went higher up the organization to ensure that she got it. "I think I was perfectly capable of doing the job but I think there was a positive factor in that one for me. There had been no woman in the job for years, and they thought it was time there was." Three staff were interviewed for the post, two men and herself. "I think that the combination of them wanting a woman in the job and the person who sponsored me for it helped me get it."

Positive action is not positive discrimination. These women were promoted through their ability, not because their organizations discriminate in favour of women. Above all, when you are discriminated against, remember the Latin motto: *Nil illegitimi carborendum* – don't let the bastards grind you down.

Advice Points
        – Official route: if the company has genuine enthusiasm for dealing with discrimination, trust the grievance procedure, but act discreetly to avoid getting a reputation as a troublemaker.
        – If discrimination against women is rife i.e. no senior women executives, consider if you want to fight or find a more encouraging atmosphere. It might be better to leave the dinosaurs to their trees.
        – If you face patronizing you could try: shock treatment: show your opinion in no uncertain terms; demonstrate

that you behave as an adult even if they behave as a child; be persistent – show them you can do the job. If the company is worth working for, senior managers should value good work over time and reward it.

– Don't allow yourself to discriminate: by employing a man because customers expect it for instance; or in the treatment of your staff, by being tougher on men and making allowances for women.

CHAPTER 7

DISCIPLINE AND CONFLICT

In all matters of opinion, our adversaries are insane – Mark
Twain.

Tradition says that men are the hunters – aggressive,
confronting the wild, bringing back the red meat,
while women are the gatherers – peacefully planti-
ng and reaping together. That stereotype has persisted
even in the highly unnatural environment of the office and
factory. Even now a woman may be branded 'hysterical' in
a workplace row, whereas a man might be admired as
'forceful' and 'having a go'. Even now many men are not
convinced that women can discipline male subordinates or
cope with confrontation.

But efforts have been made to separate the definitions of
'aggressive' and 'assertive'. Many companies and training
organizations have encouraged women to take assertiveness
courses, to overcome their natural – or perceived – inclinations

to shy away from conflict. Sometimes the old-fashioned traditionalist view even works for women. Their skills and talents in understanding, supporting and coexisting are being valued. Team working is now in vogue; coaching is recognized as better than dominating; listening has finally been accepted as a skill.

Our women managers acknowledged the real and perceived problems in disciplining their male subordinates and coping with conflict. Many of them believed that the male ego can get bruised easily – particularly when the man is coping with a woman boss. Some of them have had to deal with raw anger and they have learned how and how not to manage it.

Although some creative tension may help creative work, most of the textbook theory agrees that outright hostility has to be reduced and energy channelled into improving the work flow. One US set of solutions (Jerry Winsinski, see Further Reading) involves remembering your vowel sounds:
A – assume the person you are in conflict with means well.
E – express your feelings clearly.
I – identify what you want to happen.
O – outcome: what is expected, positive and negative aspects.
U – understanding on a mutual basis at the end of the conflict.

The actual methods used by our women managers take the theories into account and come under the following heads:
  – Prevention: better than confrontation.
  – Preparation and definition: do you know what the problem is?
  – Discussion: defining the problem with the subordinate and agreeing a solution.

84

– Diffusion: of anger, tension, defensiveness.
– Monitoring: that the solutions are working.
– Action: if solutions are not working.

Some of our interviewees have tried to duck discipline and confrontation by avoiding the problem, passing the buck upwards or sideways. However, most have found through trial and (sometimes) error how they can cope with conflict.

Prevention

The most effective way to prevent conflict and disciplinary problems is by providing an environment in which they do not arise. Establish house rules when you move into a job, or with new staff coming in. Get to know the people you are working with, make sure that they understand the rules and the fundamental discipline. If there is a problem brewing with existing staff, try to nip it in the bud. Ask them "What is troubling you?" and hit it on the head then rather than allow it to develop into something major.

The way to prevent problems then, is to lay down consistent and fair ground rules and to make sure all your staff know what they are, what they are expected to achieve, by when, and what happens if they fail or delay on work.

Preparation and Definition

If, despite attempts at prevention, you identify a problem, what then? Gail, who works in training (and has put herself on every possible training course to gain skills) once worked in the theatre, so she has learned the value of rehearsal. "I deal with any kind of conflict or disciplinary interview by being very well prepared. And I practise what I'm going to say and how."

All agreed that it is no use complaining about someone's work without being able to prove what is wrong, so it is necessary to prepare facts and figures on what has happened – that X was required to produce Y by Z and has not done so, or that the work was unacceptable for the following reasons. Without this kind of preparation the interview could turn into an 'I did', 'You didn't' slanging match. It also focuses the manager's own mind on what the problem really is and how it can be overcome.

Recognize the need for analysis: if someone is working inefficiently ask yourself Why? Are they doing a job they don't enjoy – if so can you find out what they do enjoy and could do better and move them to that type of work? Or are they working below par because they are unable to do the job properly? In which case training or coaching might be the answer. You can only resolve the problem by understanding its cause.

The Discussion
Any disciplinary interview, however informal to start with, requires a calm atmosphere. So the manager needs to ensure that the meeting takes place in private with no telephone interruptions or unexpected visitors. If you are impatient with poor performers, make a conscious effort to calm down before discussing matters with a subordinate. Cool off, then try to put yourself in their shoes to find out why they have reacted in a certain way or why they have done things wrong. Then when you talk to them, ask them their views. And if it does go as far as the disciplinary procedure try to agree checkpoints to ensure you both understand what is going to happen. Ensure that your subordinate does not leave the room without knowing what is going to happen and why. There is nothing worse than someone taking back the wrong message.

Discussion can be crucial. When something goes wrong it is important for the person to be allowed to explain it themselves, first, before you as a manager make a judgement. Then you can define the problem, the results you want and agree how to deal with it. That way you both learn.

Anita (consultant director) believed that subordinates in trouble need what she called "a bus ticket home". When she had to remove a subordinate from one job she explained why – that the client had lost confidence in him – but that there was always another point of view about events and that he would be given another chance with another client. "I'm more cautious of the male ego in these situations – men have to be seen to be in control all the time. But if someone is screwing up I'm very patient with them. I try to make sure they improve – I want them to make progress."

Gail has trained as a counsellor and emphasized the need to keep calm. "It teaches you the ability to be close but not engaged, to use reflecting skills. You repeat what they say to check both that you have understood what they have been saying and to get them to listen to what they have been saying." Sometimes this could show someone that they have exaggerated, excused or protested too much and it diffuses the tension.

A point made by many of our managers was that dealing with someone tense, shy or hostile makes solving a problem twice as difficult. So it is usually best to discuss tasks not personalities, results not personal inadequacies: "The work wasn't completed on time" rather than "You're always late".

Diffusing Anger
Gail drew on mothering as well as training skills to cope with raw anger. "I've had people towering over my desk practically spitting in my face. You don't move, you stay calm. It comes back to child rearing skills – my son throws

tantrums. Instead of letting your emotions get you, you have to persuade people to sit down and talk."

Conflict management, she said, can be difficult as people often deal with conflict as adults in the same way they did as children: through tantrums, sulking or "taking their ball away". "You have to disentangle the child's response and behave as an adult to an adult." For instance, when the subordinate accuses his manager of picking on him, the manager needs to talk reasonably about the requirements of the work.

Many women found anger hard to cope with, especially the prospect of confrontation. Often women subordinates, when criticized, react to it, show that they are mortified and want to improve. "Men are more defensive; it is almost impossible to get it through to them – perhaps because they feel insecure working for a woman."

In rare cases anger may be constructive. One of Kim's subordinates in the Civil Service is generally able but resentful of her authority. "His response is always to shout. Mine is to shout back. We clear the air and after a while we can be friends again but it is a wearing way of operating."

Beth (accountant) confounded the rules by solving a problem through unprepared confrontation. The male subordinate had been abusing the holiday system and he himself raised it in front of other staff. She responded fiercely that his behaviour was unacceptable and was surprized at the reaction. "People said they were glad I'd come down hard on him because they all knew that what he was doing was not fair."

Monitoring

After the discussion, managers need to check that the subordinate's work is improving. Exhortations to try harder do not necessarily work on their own. Sometimes it is possible to cope with the problem privately, through talking to the subordinate, working with targets, continually reviewing and monitoring. One manager holds a weekly meeting with all her staff plus half hour sessions with them individually.

Another has had considerable problems in disciplining staff as her company has no formal procedures, no recent tradition of discipline. Her subordinates were also in the habit of bypassing her, if they felt like it and appealing over her head to her boss. She has dealt with this by repeatedly pointing out to her boss that he was undermining her. He did this less as a result and so she was able to control her staff more.

Beth had problems with lack of procedures, with staff unused to discipline or deadlines. Beth's only control was through annual appraisals, which ultimately affect pay and grading. "I think because I'm a woman I do find it more difficult to discipline staff because my first instinct is always to say 'What is the problem? Let's solve it'. That does not work when someone is just lazy." However, by reviewing her staff's objectives quarterly and repeatedly emphasizing the need to keep to deadlines, she believed she was starting to change their attitude.

Action

If discussion and monitoring do not work it may be necessary to take further action. Sending someone on a training course may be an option, or transferring them to work they can cope with. If not it may be necessary to fire them. Many of our women managers had experience of this. If someone is unable to do the job, telling them helps them to perform better. You have to be quite cruel to be kind, to say "this is not working". The individual is probably very unhappy in an unsuitable job. If they acknowledge it is not working they may want to leave. Your company will almost certainly have procedures for dismissal which have to be followed. The interview itself needs to be short and above all clear, with no room for debate or delusions that the decision can be reversed. At the same time it is possible to be kind, constructive about the future and to concentrate not on personal defects but on unsuitability for the job. Some companies provide outplacement services for employees who leave – counsellors who help the employee search for a new position. This could soften the blow.

Here are five examples of how our managers have dealt with problem subordinates:

Naomi has fired people in advertising. "I've tried to do it in a straight and honest way. If what you require and what they give don't match, even when you are both trying really hard, then it is no good continuing. I've tried talking to someone in this situation, coaching, etc., but it didn't help. With conflict I try to find a way round it but in the end you have to face it, I will go to the line when it is necessary – I'm not so good when people are trying and still falling short."

Emma has had to use the disciplinary procedure once. While she was away on a legal conference someone on her staff dialled 999 with a hoax call. "As it happened I was having calls monitored because of a suspicion that one of the cleaners was telephoning abroad. One young man eventually owned up to the call. I'm not sure whether he was covering for someone else but he got a formal written warning and resigned soon afterwards."

In general she has had few disciplinary problems. "If someone makes a mistake and acknowledges it I think that's OK. If they do something gross like being drunk on duty (in the court) then they have to be disciplined. A very junior member of staff once had a verbal tussle with a member of the public which involved racist and sexist behaviour from both parties. You can't tolerate that kind of behaviour."

Tania was close to sacking a researcher who could not cope with deadlines. "He would hide material in his desk, couldn't bear to finish anything, wanted to perfect it all the time and not give it up. He also believed he knew best. I should have seen the warning signs when I recruited him. He said he was not sure he could work for a woman." He believed his expertise in the field exceeded hers in research and publishing. Finally he produced a large project late, and unpublishable. Tania had already warned her own boss that this was happening. Her boss agreed with her verdict on the work. They talked to her subordinate together and he was devastated and offered to resign. "But I chickened out on letting him go. I'd already worked out another solution, that he should swap with someone in a different department. It worked. He still argued with his new (male) boss but eventually learned to cope with deadlines and I got a good young woman into my department."

Caroline (personnel manager) made a similar mistake, taking on someone despite bad references and poor results in psychometric tests: "But I relied on the interview, which we know is the poorest form of recruitment." He turned out to be lazy and Caroline got tough, became irritated, lost her temper with him. "I would not like to have been treated the way I treated him." She put him on a performance improvement plan and a coaching plan which she made sure he followed. But he did not improve and, when she had been promoted, her successor gave him three months and told him to get another job.

Kim found it easier to discipline using formal personnel procedures. "I think the formal system protects me in that situation." She finds it more awkward having to discuss poor performance informally, one-to-one with her staff. "I think it may make it more difficult to discipline certain men because I am female and they might challenge my authority or my understanding of the situation to make the right judgment." She acknowledged that this might just be her perception rather than that of her male subordinates.

Advice Points
   –   Set ground rules and standards fairly and consistently.
   –   Check your staff understand them.
   –   If you suspect trouble is brewing deal with it early.
   –   Prepare for any disciplinary interview with facts and figures; work out what you want to achieve.
   –   Allow the subordinate to give his or her side of the story.
   –   Try to agree solutions.
   –   Keep yourself and, if possible, the subordinate, calm and focused on the problem not the personality.
   –   Monitor.
   –   If the problem continues decide on further action, e.g. training, formal disciplinary procedure, dismissal.

Avoiding Action
To avoid confrontation was a temptation to which a few of our managers succumbed, at least on specific occasions.

Margaret (biochemist) admitted to a policy of avoiding conflict at all times. "I can't think of any situations where the conflict has gone on so long that it hasn't resolved itself somehow. I step aside as much as I can."

In one instance this worked most constructively where she had to deal with a technician who was renowned for strange and aggressive behaviour: "He's a loner and extremely stubborn. You can argue with him until you're both blue in the face and it's a waste of time – he won't do as he's told." She and others sensed a repressed violence in him. "You feel he's the type to run amock with a machine gun or a machete. It's been worse when he's worked with men because they want to hit him and the conflict can escalate more violently." She coped by letting him follow his own way until he realized that his way did not work. "Then he quietly drops it and goes back to what I wanted him to do in the first place." Although she found this time consuming she has managed to get better results from him than his previous bosses.

Kim too has consciously compromised when she faces confrontation. Rather than deal directly with two of her stroppy male subordinates she bypassed them and dealt with their staff or secretaries. She, like most others preferred the friendly approach. "But my biggest problem as a manager is trying too hard to be liked and having problems getting tough when I need to do so. Early in my career a particularly bumptious male worked for me and I decided that I really had to lay down the law. He immediately started to do a take off of me as Sybil to his Basil Fawlty. I found this impossible to deal with." No management textbook could answer that one.

CHAPTER 8

SEX IN
THE OFFICE

*When a lady says no she means perhaps; when a
lady says perhaps she means yes; when a lady says yes she's no lady.*

There is a reverse quotation to the old chestnut quoted above which runs "when a businessman says yes he means perhaps..." and you can guess the rest. These quotes show the problem each sex has believing each other and why men often do not take sexual harassment seriously.

This chapter deals first with sexual harassment – what is or is not defined as harassment – how to cope as an individual and how to deal with it as a manager of someone complaining of it. After that comes sex in the office: having affairs and dealing with subordinates caught in the act.

Definitions of Sexual Harassment
Sexual harassment is unwanted conduct at work taking a sexual form – behaviour which interferes with an individual's

94

work performance or creates an intimidating, hostile or offensive working environment. Examples include:
  – Verbal advances, explicitly sexual jokes/innuen do/questions.
  – Lewd remarks or glances.
  – Physical advances.
  – Suggesting promotion or other opportunities as a reward for sexual favours (or any request for sexual favours).

Other definitions give as an example 'repeated and unwanted verbal or sexual advances', suggesting, by the use of the word 'repeated', that a one-off attempt at a chat up line might be ignored. The Equal Opportunities Commission (EOC), however, says that one serious incident is enough to constitute sexual harassment.

More and more sexual harassment policies state that harassment must be judged as such by the victim, by the impact it has on her behaviour and not by the intention of the harasser. "I didn't mean her any harm, it was just a joke" may be true but it will not wash when the effects of someone's actions lead to a distressed victim working badly as a result. So one woman might brush off sexual advances as a joke while another might find it intimidating and upsetting.

Women have also featured in harassment cases, as have men harassing men. In California a man won $1 million from a case where he said his female personnel director kissed and fondled him regularly.

Legal Penalties
Companies have good reason to discourage harassment. Victims can take their employers to an industrial tribunal for sex discrimination – for which there is now no upper limit in financial recompense, or for unfair or constructive

dismissal if the situation gets that far. A victim could also sue the perpetrator of the harassment or the employer for damage to feelings. Strathclyde Regional Council paid £3,000 to a woman for injury to feelings after two colleagues made lewd and suggestive remarks and brushed against her.

If the harasser is not the boss but a colleague, the employer could still be held liable: a tribunal could hold the company in breach of contract for not giving reasonable support to the employee who should be allowed to work without harassment or interference from colleagues.

The Metropolitan Police paid £32,000 in an out-of-court settlement to Sarah Locker who complained of sexual and racial harassment and being passed over for promotion because she was pregnant. The sexual element of the harassment included pornographic magazines being left on her desk. Even the City now takes the subject seriously. One City bank fired three men last year for allegedly making obscene suggestions to a secretary.

Over half our women managers have experienced some form of sexual harassment to themselves or subordinates. It varies from the light hearted to almost violent behaviour.

When Harassment isn't quite Harassment
Some of our women managers felt the accusation of sexual harassment could be made too lightly. One said: "These days you are getting tricky cases where I believe it's not really harassment. For instance if it's a one off – someone puts his hand up your skirt and you say 'bugger off'. I think it's only harassment if he repeats the action when you have made it quite plain that you don't want it." Other women might think that this was indecent assault.

Others describe 'being chased in the bushes' as a fond memory of youth and agree that a one-off should not count. One was in a hotel for a conference when her boss tried to kiss her. "I told him firmly to go away and fortunately he did. I didn't report him because he was so senior. I was moved on soon afterwards and we are on good terms – I lunch with him occasionally."

Aside from office party indiscretions three of our managers have been slapped on the bottom and one was grabbed at the photocopier. Questa announced that she wasn't a horse, Caroline that she wasn't a sex object. Paula yelled "sexual harassment" at the top of her voice. "You can look but you can't touch." It worked a treat. Equally effectively, Zoe waited until the offending salesman was leaving – bending over the receptionist's desk to sign out, and whacked him one back. He did not try again.

A similar technique became a fad in Rome a few years ago. Italian women, fed up with bruised backsides due to Italian men's renowned habit of pinching, started to pinch back. Whether it reduced further harassment history does not record but the women reported that the men were extraordinarily embarrassed – and the women enjoyed having their own back. Perhaps this is not to be recommended at senior management level.

Real Harassment
The advice points on page 102 give the steps that should be taken to deal with sexual harassment. But many of our women managers have found it difficult to confront.

Minor forms can still upset the recipient, or just be a permanent irritant. Olivia (engineer) became annoyed at page three calendars decorating one colleague's office. "I found it not so much offensive as unnecessary." He obviously recognized it as at least partially offensive as he took them down when his or anyone else's wife came to the office.

More seriously, another colleague of Olivia's harassed most of the women who worked for him. "The trouble was he was studying law in his spare time and he knew exactly how far he could go." She and other colleagues found it impossible to gather evidence. In another instance a manager had to endure more hands-on harassment – particularly hairstroking from one boss in her early days at work. "Then I laughed embarrassedly and avoided him when I could. Now I'd say straight off that I didn't expect to be stroked at work and I don't like it."

A typical exchange concerned a manager who suffered constant harassment in an early job in manufacturing where she was the only woman manager in an almost all male company of 700. The culture was booze and sex, down the pub every evening and passes made at the annual do: threats like "if you don't sleep with me bad things will happen." She says of a product launch: "There would be dry ice and girls in tiny tops and crotch skimming mini skirts virtually stripping on stage – met with whistles and sexist jokes." Eventually she found it "too sordid and revolting; I was fed up with trailblazing in a company going nowhere so I got out."

Harriet (managing director of a consultancy) occasionally had to deal with sexual innuendo from potential or actual clients. She believed she must assume that the man had genuine feelings of attraction and should not be repulsed to the extent of hurting him. "When you're selling, if you're really looking after your business interest you can't bruise their ego. But if you can maintain respect for the person you can handle it."

However, she almost failed to handle a man who worked for her inside the firm who tried to assault her. She had thought he was under control, despite a mild flirtation, but was wrong. "I allowed myself to be alone with him and it was a huge mistake. I thought that I had preserved his feelings, that the fire was out. I was wrong." She felt partly at fault for the flirtation so did not report it.

The most serious cases of harassment came from Sarah (estate agent). In a previous job her manager pinched and grabbed her. When she told him not to he became aggressive. To cope: "I just gladly accepted assignments to get out of the way. I was very depressed (from changing jobs) and I became isolated." To manage her own team and avoid her boss she worked by telephone and short meetings. "I was managing by remote control – it was chaotic." She survived to build her team into a successful unit but moved on, partly for other reasons.

In her current job she was caught in a complicated power struggle and, while trying to resolve the conflict, was again subjected to sexual harassment. She had to work with a senior manager who was hostile to new ideas being introduced. "I tried to invite him into the work I was doing so that we could work as a team. I tried to back him in what he was doing to show I could be flexible and he misunderstood. He was having marriage difficulties and hinted he would like a relationship with me."

She was horrified but the more she insisted that the relationship should stay professional, the more pointed his comments became. Finally he became physical, pinching and pinging her bra strap and blowing on her neck while she was on the telephone to clients. On that occasion a male colleague ordered him off. She realized he was offensive to other women staff and finally warned the group managing director what was happening and that she intended to tackle the offender. Sarah gave him leaflets on sexual harassment and explained clearly why she and other women in the office found his words and actions unpleasant. He started to behave better with the others but not with her. Finally he turned nasty, referred to her as the token crumpet and tried to undermine her work. She was by now terrified to be alone with him, in a car or the office.

Her husband encouraged her to fight but finally she put in her resignation. Her boss, supportive but seemingly unable to control the harasser, refused to accept it. The offender has since left. Sarah felt she could have done more to prevent the harassment andresolved that no one would be allowed to do this with her own charges.

Dealing with Harassed Subordinates
Ranee (doctor) has been in the middle of sexual harassment problems. "The one serious case was a junior doctor who was working his way round all the other junior female medical staff. He became very heavy with them, some were quite intimidated." Fortunately, one woman started discussing his behaviour and all the others said "he did that to me too".

The harassment came out because they were all living in residency together and this helped with dealing with the culprit. "We all completely ignored him – the men supported us too; no one socialized with him at all." Those who had been intimidated felt supported and he learned not to try it on again.

In a more conventional office setting many of our women managers found it easier dealing with subordinates' problems than their own. Gail (TV, working in training and HR) advised firmness with the offender and boosting the assertiveness of the victim. "Mostly the harassers are male and white," she said. She has dealt with cases of racial and sexual harassment. "I deal with it initially by telling them the victim is entitled to professional respect."

Another told the victims to be firm, to show that the man's attentions were not welcome. "So many times I've seen the man thinking that if he asks enough times the women will roll over. Lots of men don't actually believe in sexual harassment."

Even when procedures are followed and the culprit is dealt with, he may not change. One of our managers helped a colleague (while working in Australia) who was being harassed. While they went through procedures a female colleague of the victim also alleged harassment. Her husband threatened to sue so the board reached an agreement with the culprit to leave. Years later, in England, our manager met a woman in another company complaining of harassment by the same man.

Women as Harassers
One or two of the interviewees admitted to a minor form of harassing men – at least flirting and teasing, more often with colleagues and clients although one suggested "power might be part of it". One other had been informally accused of sexual harassment which seemed, she thought, to be based on pique. After working closely and successfully with a colleague she believed the sexual chemistry between them was about to ignite. Not wanting a relationship at work she drew back. He was bewildered and finally angry.

Her boss later told her the man had complained of sexual harassment although he (the boss) had not believed it. When she later confronted the man he denied complaining about her. "I'm a lot more careful with him now."

101

Advice Points
If you are a victim:
  – Make a written note of the offensive behaviour with dates, times, any witnesses.
  – If you can, say straight away, politely, that you do not find the behaviour acceptable or conducive to work.
  – Even if you are taken aback the first time, rehearse what you could say if it happens again.
  – Try a written complaint to the offender.
  – Discreetly check with your female peers – whether he has harassed them.
  – The EOC advises that even if the unwanted behaviour stops you should inform someone in authority. You may not be the only sufferer and your employers cannot help if they do not have the facts.

If the behaviour continues you could:
  – Take up any grievance/harassment procedure with the company.
  – If there isn't one, ask a friend/colleague to go with you to the offender and discuss it (again make notes).
  – Go to personnel/trade unions/your boss (if he is not the culprit; to his boss if he is).
  – If the culprit is the owner of the company go to the Citizens' Advice Bureau.
  – Take notes at each stage and check that your complaint is being dealt with and action is taken.
  – If the harassment creates stress or otherwise injures you, go to your doctor. As well as the help she may provide, the doctor may also give evidence of your condition.
  – If no action is taken and the behaviour persists you can claim sex discrimination or victimization. You can get advice from the EOC but, to take your case to an industrial tribunal, you must lodge the complaint with the

Central Office of Industrial Tribunals within three months less one day from the date of the act of which you complained.

— To start proceedings, get an IT1 form from the EOC or a Jobcentre and send it to the Central Office of Industrial Tribunals.

— New regulations mean that if the tribunal agrees, the case does not receive any publicity until a conclusion is reached.

If you are managing someone who alleges harassment:
— Take the complaint seriously; do not laugh it off. Even small firms have a duty to take steps to prevent harassment.

— Follow any company procedures.

— If there are none, discuss the complaint anonymously (i.e. not revealing the victim's or the culprit's name) with personnel or appropriate senior manager.

— If you are met with disbelief or unconcern, point out the potential cost of a court case and the harm done to the work of the individual.

— See if your competitor companies operate harassment policies or provide confidential counselling services (British Gas and Whitbread have introduced internal counsellors for instance) and point this out to your senior management.

— Let the victim know what you are doing, when and why.

— Discreetly check with others whether the culprit is harassing other women.

— If the complaint cannot be solved informally, make sure that it is investigated impartially with both sides putting their case, with a friend if they want.

If the complaint is proved:
— Put no pressure on the victim to transfer: this can

be offered, but she should not be forced. The offender should be transferred instead.

    – Check afterwards that the woman is not victimized by colleagues or other managers.

Further Information
Equal Opportunities Commission
Overseas House, Quay Street,
Manchester M3 3HN
Tel: 0161 833 9244
Scotland:
EOC,
Stock Exchange House,
7 Nelson Mandela Place,
Glasgow G2 1QW
Tel: 0141 248 5833
Wales:
EOC,
Caerways House,
Windsor Lane,
Cardiff CF1 1LB
Tel: 01222 343552

The National Association of Citizens' Advice Bureaux
Myddleton House, Pentonville Road,
London N1 9LZ
Tel: 0171 833 2181 (will provide list of local CABs)

Women Against Sexual Harassment
312 The Chandlery, 50 Westminster Bridge Road,
London SE1 7QY
Tel: 0171 721 7592 (support network)

Office Affairs – Why Not?
The consensus about sex in the office was "Don't". Gail (training manager) explained why.

"I met Hamish when I was an inexperienced personnel manager in local government in Scotland. He was my boss and utterly charismatic: piercing blue eyes, very powerful, very manipulative. It was the only time in 20 years I have had a relationship with someone at work.

"It was wonderful at the time but looking back it was sexual harassment. He would sit me on his lap, chase me round the desk and I didn't mind. However, it taught me never to do it again. It impacts on your work, reduces your objectivity, removes clarity and sidetracks you from your own career path. It undermines your professional persona – not the man's; colleagues just say 'here he goes again' but they think that you are not serious. They may still see you as nice and intelligent but it undermines your credibility."

For Gail this was emphasized when she ended the affair, amicably, and Hamish started a new relationship with someone else in the office. "I listened to what they said about her and realized that they must have talked about me in the same way."

Others agreed that men and women are perceived and treated differently when affairs are discovered. The man may be covertly admired while the woman, sometimes even by other women, is regarded as loose and unprofessional. Senior managers tend to deal with the problem (if they see it as such) by moving or firing the woman and having a cautionary word with the man. The reason given is usually that the man is in a more important position and the woman is more expendable.

Anita (consultant director) has seen this happen in a variety of companies. "The cardinal rule is that when it blows up the woman goes and the man stays. Early on in my career I had a boss who was a bit nifty with his hands and he attacked his secretary. She left, he was moved."

Zoe and Yvonne were both involved in unhappy marriages when they embarked on office affairs. In Zoe's case, when the affair was discovered, she was summoned by the managing director who told her that he had discussed it with the man she was seeing and they had both decided that she should leave as she was earning less money. She forgave the man this high-handed treatment and later lived with him. In Yvonne's case her boss gave her the bad news: she had to leave, not the man.

Isobel (librarian) herself took the option to leave when she was about to marry her future husband who worked in the same office.

Although these days blind eyes are turned more frequently to relationships developing between professionals, it does seem that affairs can upset the people around, creating minor jealousies and hiccups in the work. Our women managers, even those who had indulged on occasion, almost unanimously felt it was better to sin away from one's own doorstep if possible.

Beth, the accountant, went further than this. "Most people who have power and influence are in their 40s and 50s and when I worked in a previous firm there were lots of young, unattached women, some of them sexually adventurous. The men exercized their power and the women found it attractive to be with men who were rich and powerful." She felt this coloured the men's perception of all women at work, to the detriment of those who wanted to be taken seriously.

She and others also felt that relationships distracted men (in one case her boss) and women from doing their jobs properly. "That particular boss was totally distracted and not able to give his full attention to his job or running the pastoral side of his role as a manager. He completely wrecked the group's atmosphere."

On the Other Hand...
Where else do you meet people? Many aspiring women managers concentrate most of their life on their work and several of our interviewees met their current partners at work or on training courses for work .

Harriet, who runs her own business, admitted to affairs with her staff. "It's the only place I meet people – it's that or being a nun. It's very difficult and it's detrimental to the relationship – you have to make an effort not to touch in the office." She found the separation of the two roles hard to cope with but necessary to preserve because of the others in the office who would be embarrassed if the relationship were known.

When a relationship ended she found it even more difficult. She tended to avoid the man for a while: "There's a lot of tension and everyone feels very uncomfortable. Then you reach a point when you are slightly more comfortable and eventually the ideal is to become friends. The problem with that is that it is often misinterpreted that you want to start the affair again. Even if you tell them that, the male tends not really to believe it."

At one stage she was running two affairs. "You have to balance enjoying the game and respecting everyone's feelings. You keep them apart and you hope they don't talk to each other. If they do, you risk losing both." While all was kept secret, she said, it did no harm to the business. On the contrary, everyone was very committed to work. But she accepted that one slip and the work as well as relationships would be badly damaged. However, she insisted that she did not want to become a recluse. "I keep them all in separate compartments. But you have to remember which one you are in all the time and not forget or drink too much."

Harriet's reaction to a subordinate having affairs was to advise them to be careful, to compartmentalize and to remember which hat they were wearing. Advice from others would be: Don't.

Dealing with Subordinates' Affairs

Emma (lawyer) had to face the problem with two juniors having an affair in her office. "With hindsight I think I allowed myself to become too involved in the welfare role in giving advice. The boy was moved to another department." This makes a change from the traditional solution.

Ranee found that in hospitals relationships did develop, between nurses and doctors and between doctors. "It sometimes gets in the way of work but mostly people are quite professional about it." Ranee became stuck in the middle of one hospital affair. Starting a new job as a registrar she found out her consultant, who was in the middle of a divorce, had been having an affair with his secretary and was starting a new one with one of Ranee's junior doctors.

She became the shoulder the consultant cried on, because he needed emotional support during his divorce. The secretary wanted her support too at the break up of the affair and meanwhile she had to manage the junior doctor which was quite hard because she had a direct link to the consultant.

"I think you just try to ignore it on the whole because if it's not directly affecting the care of the patients and as long as the job is getting done – and it was – there's no harm being done. She was actually a good junior doctor. The problem was the gossip generated within the unit." Gossip may not only be disruptive to work. In a case last year two staff in a bank were found unfairly dismissed. Known as the 'Sex on a desk' case, a cleaner alleged that she found the two making love on a desk. They were fired with, according to the tribunal, no opportunity given to them to put their case and their evidence.

Paula (finance controller) once worked for a man who was having an affair with one of her staff. He finished it, which made Paula's subordinate very resentful, and promptly started a new liaison with another of her staff. "I coped by working around and not to him," she said. "There were scenes in the office between the two women. I had to divide up the ex and the new so that they didn't come into contact. Everyone knew what he was doing but no one did anything about it. He's still there."

Advice Points
As an individual:
          – Office affairs are exciting but ... consider:
                    The effects on your work;
                    The effects on your reputation.
Will you be taken seriously by your peers or senior management if they find out?

As a manager:
          – It is only your business if an affair affects your or your subordinates' work.
                    – If the affair affects your subordinates' performance:
                    Talk to the individuals concerned;
                    Point out the effects on their work colleagues;
                    Suggest they modify behaviour to change
                    this;

Warn that if there is no change you may have
to invoke the disciplinary procedure.
– If your boss is having an affair with your
subordinate:
Consider a quiet talk with your boss explaining
the effect of his/her behaviour on work and
morale within the department;
Point out to him/her the difficulties
you face, caught in the middle;
Point out the problems to your subordinate –
how the affair is affecting work.
– If the above has no effect and work is being seriously disrupted you may have to consider talking to personnel or your boss's boss, despite the potential risk to your
position.

CHAPTER 9

WORK AND FAMILIES

Good employers know that it pays to adapt to family commitments – Ann Widdecombe, (Employment Minister, 1994.)

But how many of them do? A 1992 study found that only about 8% of employers in the private sector give childcare provision and that childcare vouchers were given by 55 organizations in the public sector and 70 companies.

In the UK 60% of couples with children have both partners working. Our women managers admitted that, in their life, responsibility for care of the home and the children was ultimately theirs, not their husbands'. So women bear the childcare burden as well as that of a full time job.

In this chapter we show how they coped – both with managing their families and their colleagues' and bosses' perception of working wives and mothers. Some of the

111

attitudes they have faced have been nakedly hostile, showing yet again that a minority of men still believe women
should get back to the kitchen.

Self Help
If you can get help with childcare in your own company it
makes your working life easier. If you cannot, are you in a
position where you could campaign for or initiate some
form of scheme? Below is a list of childcare provisions/aids
to managing work and family with some examples of companies that use them. These could be good for propaganda
while lobbying the personnel department.

Parental leave – example: three months' leave for either parent to be taken between the end of maternity leave and the
baby's second birthday. An EU directive proposed this 11
years ago. The Equal Opportunities Commission (EOC)
suggested it would cost 0.01% of the pay bill.

Some UK examples:
Better than statutory maternity leave: Penguin Books – 25
weeks after one year's service. British Gas and British
Telecom – three months.

Paternity leave: IPC Magazines – two weeks. Channel 4 –
three weeks.

Adoption leave: National Westminster Bank – up to six
months unpaid for one parent if both work for the Bank.
Littlewoods – six weeks at 90% pay.

Family leave: days off to cope with child's illness, etc.
Penguin Books up to 15 days paid. Lloyds Bank up to four
weeks.

Career breaks: range from two to five years unpaid with

some regular training/contact. Most of the high street banks have good schemes, as does Marks & Spencer. Can operate cheaply in small companies.

Job sharing: also cheap for employers. The banks do it, plus British Gas and British Telecom plus many public sector organizations. Further information from New Ways To Work (Tel. 0171 226 4026).

Workplace nurseries: even a small firm could take some places in an existing nursery. For examples, try the Workplace Nurseries Campaign (Tel. 0171 700 0281).

Childcare allowances: Penguin Books, Institute of Personnel and Development.

Childcare vouchers: not subject to National Insurance contributions (for examples call Childcare Vouchers Ltd, (Tel. 0171 834 6666).

Out of school provision: schemes for after school and holidays. Try your local authority, the National Out of School Alliance (Tel. 0171 247 3009) and the National Playing Fields Association (Tel. 0171 584 6445).

Flexible hours/working from home: cheap for the employer, no pay lost by staff. Increasingly popular in banks, retail, etc. although less likely to be available for senior staff.

Practically all the above schemes normally apply to fathers as well as mothers, so you might gain support from male colleagues as well as female.

Losing Confidence?
One problem of returning to work after maternity leave is loss of confidence. Formal career break schemes avoid this

by keeping in contact, providing days or weeks of training. However, even if you return after six months or less it helps to keep in touch, pop into work, keep up with the network and the gossip.

Diane (product manager) did those things during her pregnancies but still had problems getting back. "I'd been getting all my mail at home, had paid attention to what was going on and generally kept myself visible. But I do feel a loss of confidence now I'm back. That may be through lack of sleep with the baby waking me most nights. Or because of the changes – I don't know what's going on and no one is going to sit down and fill you in."

Jean (chief executive) agreed that most women do lose confidence – but after she had her second child she did a course at the Open University. "It made me realize I could think, I could talk, that I had a head on my shoulders for communicating and debating – it was wonderful – a breath of fresh air." It restored her confidence. Although she said she had not, in fact, become too downhearted she found that returning did involve a certain amount of nervousness: had the organization changed much, could she do the job?

Some sort of part time course or intellectual stimulus at least prevents the feeling that Diane had while on maternity leave – that she was a nonentity or non–person with a pram. Most mothers of small babies seem to experience this for a time, particularly when they have little adult companionship. Work restores the feeling that you still have a brain and most of our women managers got to grips within a few weeks. In fact Diane was so angry with her boss during her first maternity leave because of his assumption that mums don't work she flung herself back into full time work: "I worked my socks off to prove him wrong."

114

Perceptions of Pregnancy

A few found that their senior managers, usually older men, were embarrassed by the fact of their pregnancy. Younger subordinates and peers were generally more enthusiastic about it and Beth said her clients were happy for her and encouraging – unlike her boss. "The clients thought it was marvellous for someone to have the drive and determination to keep going."

Anita applied for her first management job knowing she was pregnant and told her new employers only when she was seven months. "The Employment Protection (Consolidation) Act 1976 and the Sex Discrimination Act were my saviours – without them I would not be sitting here now." She took over from someone who was retiring but she knew he would like to continue part time. She arranged work so that he could do part of her job, she could cope with some at home. She then presented the plan to her boss as a packaged solution. "The manager who had appointed me had three kids and he said 'Fine'!"

Perceptions on Return

Most of our working mothers were keen to prove themselves just as competent as before. One told us: "There is a problem that if you go home at 4pm to be there when your child comes home you feel you have to prove to male colleagues that you are not swanning off. It's partly me, my problem. They think they have got to be there all hours, so I'm imagining that they are thinking that I'm not committed or keen enough." She believed she was less committed than male colleagues to the job itself and described her commitment as self interest – she was prepared to work long and hard but only on her objectives set by her boss. She, like others, worried about others' perceptions of the hours she worked and felt guilty taking time off.

Some senior managers showed disapproval when the women returned to work. The implication was that if women worked they were failed mothers, and if they were mothers they were bound to be failures at work. Our women managers coped by proving to peers and bosses that their work was as good as it was before.

Working Patterns

Diane now works four days a week. Beth works flexitime which she finds a boon. Harriett and Jean both control their working hours flexibly. Gail returned to work full time at first but six months later reduced this to three days a week. "There was a major crisis when I went for promotion. They said five days a week; I said four with one day when I'm available but not necessarily at work. I was a single mum then and I needed that option. It took three months to negotiate. The problem is that part time is equated with part committed. The director said 'I know you can do it but there is a perception that you can't on a four day week'. I said 'whose perception? We have a part time chairman, a director who is a JP and takes time off for that'. 'That', he said, 'was different'."

Another had a similar experience. She worked part time until her child was eight then joined a company which insisted she should work full time. "More fool them – I would have done just as much of the work part time as full time, putting in extra hours at home." She had childcare help from a partner when her child was younger. Some of our women managers have child-minders, some have live-in nannies. Many talked about the difficulties of travelling on business. Nannies are invaluable when flights are delayed or when you have to work late. But the family always comes first in an emergency.

One manager who was married to a lecturer when her

children were young and got a lot of help from him, took a job some way from home. "I left home at 7am and got back at 7pm. It was unfair on the kids and on my husband so I left after a few months."

Another felt initially discriminated against when she returned to work, allocated the worst jobs. She accepted, however, that this could have been because she was not prepared to do extensive travel. "I was happy to go away for two or three days or the odd week but not for weeks on end."

Cost

Beth pointed out that the cost of childcare is high. "It is a really significant factor when I assess my next career move. If I am going to get on I am going to have to work in London – all the best jobs are there. But the economics are horrendous. With three young children I need a qualified nanny – £180 a week or £250 in London or more." In practice, she felt, that way of developing her career was barred to her because of the cost.

Support from Spouses

Helpful husbands and partners, said most, were an important factor in combining work and family. The women themselves seemed to accept that the primary responsibility for childcare should be theirs – one has a husband who was a brilliant cook and able to run dinner parties. (Why is it that husbands help by doing the interesting jobs?)

Those married women without children also cited help from partners. Linda frequently worked a 12 hour day. "My husband works for himself. He is a modern man – shares the cooking, walks the dog. But the buck still stops with me domestically. I pay the bills, do the lion's share of domestic work."

Vanessa (public service organization) like many others, put family first. Married to someone in the same organization but in a different department, she was concerned when her promotion left him two grades behind. "I thought it might create a problem but it didn't. If it had I would have left. I would not lose a wonderful relationship for just a job."

Managing Kids – Managing Men
Both Anita and Gail made parallels between dealing with small children and recalcitrant men at work. Anita compared a board of directors with a children's party. Gail said: "The parenting process is very enlightening on management. While I don't think you can treat every man as a six-year-old it does help sometimes." She believed small girls are manipulative, small boys straightforward. "With all kids you have to slow down and be clear about the task you want done. Then you have to put in quality control checks and monitor. If a six-year-old falls off his bike, the first time you put him back on. He does it again, you put him back and explain why. The third time you take the bike away for a few seconds to get his attention and say 'You'll go on falling off unless you do this. Are you going to do this?' Then he will either not fall off – or not tell you about it."

She and Anita (both from personnel backgrounds) described it as a mechanical breaking down of a process. Sometimes it is necessary to take their bike away to get their attention and give it back when they have understood the rules. "Mind you," said Gail, "with some people you're always putting them back on their bike."

Advice Points
  – Press for family-friendly personnel policies at work.
  – Keep in touch while away on maternity leave; maintain visibility and involvement.

- Negotiate appropriate hours/time off to maintain a balance between work and the family.
- Balance the cost of childcare against long-term career plans; extra expenditure in the short term may easily repay itself in career progression.
- Use experience gained in raising children to manage at work.

CHAPTER 10

TO MANAGE OR NOT TO MANAGE

In some cases, setting up a business is a woman's only option as a result of age, discrimination, redundancy or the difficulties of combining a career and children – Pauline Hyde – Chair, Lee Hecht Hamson (Europe) – outplacement consultancy.

Our A to Z of women managers reveal themselves as thoughtful, progressive and positive – but not power hungry for power's sake. Although a few aspire to the chief executive role, even they are looking beyond that, thinking of different roles in the future, different types of job satisfaction from different work.

In times of recession and altering styles of employment (i.e. more emphasis on short-term contracts, high management turnover, job restructuring) it makes sense for every manager to consider alternative roles should change be thrust upon them.

In this chapter we look at the alternatives considered and

120

why, the pros and cons of job security and finally the best bits of being a manager – what makes it worth while.

Freelancing
You may consider moving into freelance work:
 – After a career break, as a means of getting back into work part time.
 – To run your own working life.
 – To increase the variety in your work.
 – As a means of continuing to work if full time permanent employment in your speciality is declining or unavailable.
 – To build a professional reputation, widening your expertize and contacts for jobs in the future.
 – As a start in ultimately running your own business.

Freelancing may seem an attractive option – no more commuting time/costs, no more sandwich-bar lunches, you can wear jeans (practically) every day, watch soaps at lunchtime and play with the cat. However, it does not provide financial security. Working alone requires self-discipline and when things go wrong, can be miserable. Freelances miss the friendliness of an office and learning through bouncing ideas off others and formal training programmes. Clients expect your skills to be as up-to-date as their new office technology.

Two of the interviewees have gone freelance. Gail (training manager in TV) believed there is a functional glass ceiling in her company. She would have to move into general management to be promoted. "So I'm going freelance. After 15 years I think it's time to put myself at risk. Risk is a form of renewal – I want to explore. I plan to do two years as a freelance and then review the situation. If it's fun and I earn enough money I'll really go for it, turn it into a proper

business with other people working for me." If not her contacts are probably good enough to put her straight back in a
TV company or elsewhere for a change.

Another freelance has never regretted it. Occasionally she
finds the self-discipline of working alone hard to cope with.
She misses training people, seeing them develop and sometimes misses the camaraderie of office life. "But I don't
miss working for idiots, pretending they're not idiots. I
don't miss office politics, the rush hour."

Both have swapped ambition for autonomy, control over
others for control over their own lives. They have also
swapped paid holidays, sick leave, etc. for unpaid. They
pay for their own training, pensions and their own perks.
They do their own administration – no more secretaries,
receptionist to take messages, boss to rely on. Freelances
have to create good relations with a variety of clients so
they have swapped one boss for many. But the relationship
is different working for clients.

In employment you generally report to one person – as a
freelance you are likely to have many clients. If you have
problems with your boss, you might have to change your
job; if you have difficulties with a client, at least that should
not affect your overall employment. Generally, clients treat
you with greater respect – you and they know that either
party can vote with their feet. "You can't always choose
your work when there isn't much around but at least it provides variety".

Own Business
Successful freelancing can result in too much business for
one person to handle. Rather than turn away work, a successful freelance may wish to grow her own business. In
certain professions/occupations, being a freelance is not an

option: e.g. setting up a shop, a solicitor's office, an estate agency. There are greater burdens in running a business than freelancing: premises, employees, tax and legal implications.

Most businesses require staff – at least part of the time – and that brings us back to management but with much greater responsibility and control than in ordinary employment.

The financial responsibility and commitment may also be much greater. It can be extremely difficult to separate work from personal life.

Harriet currently runs her own business. The attraction was flexibility, working hours and control over what she put in and got out. The drawbacks were lack of financial security and lack of the support you get from a large organization. "It can be lonely. I find I segment the time when I work alone and when I go out and sell." She finds it particularly hard to divide her time between her family and her business. "I think it's impossible to do either as well as you would want to do. You always feel that you are not giving your work or your family enough. You are letting either your family or your business down."

There is also the problem of delegating and covering when she is away – on business or holiday. After a recent three week business trip she returned to find her deputy had not been able to cope. Clients were unhappy at the standard of service and new opportunities had been missed. Despite the drawbacks she believes that the ability to control her own life makes it worth while.

Jean has run her own business twice – the first time managing women only. She helped two other women set up a franchise for one of the major recruitment chains in the early 1980s. "It was boom time, we had such a successful first year." But after three years she found the all-women atmosphere stifling and moved out. "I remember an all-female conference where the loo was just a haze of lacquer. It was horrendous. All frilly women and frilly girls."

Later in the 1980s she ran a publishing company producing two magazines. She saw the benefits as: "Financial management, financial control, flexibility. In its heyday I employed six people plus freelances. They were good years." She was able to put into practice ideas that she would have welcomed as an employee. For instance, she allowed staff to take a 'catch up' day off per month, in addition to holidays, because it was a perk she would have enjoyed when her children were small.

The disadvantages were: "You never leave it. My home and office were in the same village." She found herself popping in at weekends, unable to divorce work from home.

The business prospered until the recession of 1990. When the slow decline started to look fatal she warned her staff and suggested they should look for jobs. The village pensioners who packed the magazines offered to work for free. That showed that treating staff well pays off. The business still folded but she remembers her team of staff with affection.

Advice Points – Freelancing
     – Can you work from home? Do you have the space and facilities, i.e. telephone, office area, desk and other equipment?
     – Consider where, how this would affect partner/children. Can you create a professional environment when clients telephone/call?

To Manage or Not to Manage?

- Can you afford to make the break in one go? It helps to have at least one regular contract before leaving the security of full time employed work.
- Can you price your work realistically? Check on others in your field. Do not be afraid to charge different employers/clients different amounts. Are you going to charge by the hour, the day or the quantity of work?
- Have you considered: paid holidays and who covers for you? Sick leave and who covers for you?
- In your field can you keep your skills up-to-date? Can you afford the time and/or money?
- Can you afford to pay for a personal pension? For medical insurance? A car?
- Do you have the contacts and ability to promote yourself to attract new clients? Planning for the future, even when you are busy, is essential to avoid unpaid gaps.
- Don't immediately buy expensive equipment that you can't afford. Wait until you have enough regular work that requires it; i.e. an old dressing table can become a desk and you don't need a laser printer to send out speculative letters.
- Find a reliable accountant, by recommendation, and take advice on tax and accounts management. For instance, you may get tax reductions on heating, telephone bills, etc.

Advice Points – Starting Up a Business
See above, plus:
The additional problems of running your own business are:
- Whether to set up as a sole trader, partnership, or as a company limited or otherwise: the legal and tax implications.
- Premises: can the business be run from home, garage or not?
- Staff: does the business need full time, part time, temporary or contract staff?

125

- Local, national and European laws, governing premises (planning permission, etc.), VAT, health and safety, employment (maternity, sick pay, contracts, NI, sex and race discrimination, pensions, etc.).

Sources of Information

Planning permission – local council.

Employment law– Department of Employment – try the Jobcentre and Equal Opportunities Commission (see page 104) and the Commission for Racial Equality (Tel. 0171 828 7022).

Health and Safety – Health and Safety Executive (Secretariat: Tel. 0171 243 6000).

VAT – HM Customs & Excise (local offices).

National Insurance – Department of Social Security (local offices).

Pensions – National Association of Pension Funds (Tel. 0171 730 0585).

General – relevant employers' association.

Pipe Dreams

"I'd love to be someone's mother," said Sarah (the estate agent), although her boss was pushing hard for her to take over his job as a director. "He says he's going to take a sabbatical so that I'm forced to do it." Other long-term ambitions were: "I'd love to write something. I'd like to go back into education – I understand the value now of 'A' levels which I didn't when I dropped them. I would really like to do something for society. I'd like to pay back. If I were not married with a good career I'd probably be in Bosnia helping street kids."

Paula (finance controller) was also concerned that her boss was pushing her to move up too fast. "He's growing me for his job, say in two or three years' time. It doesn't necessarily bother me – going up the scale. You can make just as big a business impact at other levels, on the business, on people. You can get job satisfaction at any level so I don't want a job that's beyond me, I don't want to fall over and struggle. I want to contribute but go on enjoying it."

Eventually, though, she would like to go on the board, provided the work stays interesting. "I don't need to play power games – I never have. I've got where I am in four years here without doing so. I don't compromise. But in 10 years time I would like to give it all up and do something completely different – like open a cattery."

Naomi has the same sort of idea. "I've changed from wanting to be managing director to wanting to be more creative." In advertising for all her career she sometimes wondered about all the fuss created over the packaging of a box of peanuts. It was then that she thought about importing and selling New Zealand pottery. "I want to make a difference to things I value, that might last and are beautiful. I would be working for myself not for a lot of money or even autonomy but to do something worthwhile." On the other hand, she said, when she checked on customer satisfaction in her current company, or opened the eyes of senior managers to something new, she felt she was doing something worthwhile.

Doubts about the Top

Several managers indicated their reluctance to aim for the very top. "I don't have any desire to go higher, you just get hassle. I prefer the technical side," said one. She would not risk financial insecurity by moving to self employment but had no plans to aim for the company boardroom.

Fiona, the editor, too had doubts about ambition. "I always thought I did want to be a manager, and the secret of solving the problems might be to go higher but the problem is, I think, that you waste such a lot of time." She found the stress was like being a parent again. "There's nothing to show for being a parent or a manager because what you do is build good relationships rather than anything physical.

"If you stay at home and bring up your children and they turn into model citizens you have to wait 20 years to find out and even then it may have nothing to do with you." She felt that managing was the same – putting effort and energy in and frequently getting back aggravation. "If you put that energy into something more focused, you might achieve more in terms of money or other satisfaction." So she is considering self employment with a wary eye on the financial risks.

The Benefits
These three were, however, in the minority. Most of the others enjoyed the process of managing. Although work may be frustrating when it goes wrong, the highs more than made up for it.

Vanessa (manager in public service) said: "The best thing is when people say thank you. I'm responsible for career development and I got an unexpected Christmas card saying how much someone who worked for me appreciated my fighting battles for them."

Emma, the lawyer, did not see herself as a natural manager. "I'm not always comfortable with the role. There are boundaries set by the culture and constraints of the organization, so that one is never operating according to one's own standards. But I would not have missed it for anything. I like the people and the personnel side of management. I love being a member of selection and promotion boards. I need the structure of an organization in which to work during the week and I like the family atmosphere.

Non–financial rewards are very important: the friendship, the gossip, the feeling of belonging."

Kim, in the Civil Service also rated the people factor highly. "I've never considered radical alternatives as I suspect I like the security of working in a big organization – not that it is as secure these days as it used to be. I do enjoy being a manager and I think it is one of the things that I do best in my current job. I would very much not want to move to a job where I gave up management responsibilities. I think I like managing people because I am basically nosey about them and I do like the personal interaction. I also like having staff to do the tedious work for me so that I can get on with the interesting stuff."

Like some of the others Kim wanted job satisfaction rather than the kudos of the top job. "It is possible that politics can get you to the top in some organizations and I suspect my unwillingness to get involved reflects the fact that I'm not sure that the top is where I want to be. I am much more interested in doing a job I enjoy, one that brings job satisfaction, rather than in the hassle and pressure of moving further up the tree."

Anita, consultant director, relished her career. "The best bit of managing is when your subordinates realize that it's working – when they are doing a very difficult, highly political report and they say that you have opened windows for them, enabled them to work with each other and achieve things, when they can work out how to make progress."

Naomi summed it up. "Work provides a stimulus – and managing is fun."

FURTHER READING

Meredith Belbin: *Team Roles at Work*, Butterworth-Heinemann (Oxford), 1993.

Warren Bennis: *Leaders: The Strategies for Taking Charge*, Harper & Row (New York), 1985.

Robert Bramson: *Coping with Difficult Bosses*, Nicholas Brealey Publishing (London), 1993.

D Clutterbuck: *Everyone Needs a Mentor*, IPM (London), 1985.

Liz Curtis: *Making Advances – what you can do about sexual harassment at work*, BBC Books (London), 1991.

Daniel Dana: *Talk It Out*, Kogan Page (London), 1991.

Marilyn J Davidson and Cary L Cooper: *Shattering the Glass Ceiling – the woman manager*, Paul Chapman Publishing (London), 1992.

Peter Drucker: *Management for Results*, Heinemann (Oxford), 1989, latest edition 1994.

Martin Edwards: *How to Get the Best Deal From Your Employer*, Kogan Page (London), 2nd edition 1991.

Veronica Groocock: *Women Mean Business*, Ebury Press (London), 1988.

Charles Handy: *The Age of Unreason*, Arrow Business Books (London), 1989; *Gods of Management*, Souvenir Press (London), 1986; *Understanding Organisations*, Penguin Harmondsworth (London), 1993; *The Empty Raincoat*,

Hutchinson (London), 1994.

Colin Hastings, Peter Bixby, Rani Chaudhry-Lawton: *The Superteam Solution*, Ashridge/Gower Publishing (Aldershot), 1986.

Robert Heller: *The Complete Guide to Modern Management*, Mercury Press (London), 1991.

Rosabeth Moss Kanter: *When Giants Learn to Dance*, Simon & Schuster (London), 1989; *The Change Masters*, George Allen & Unwin (London), 1984; *Men and Women of the Corporation*, Basic Books (New York), 1993.

Paul Kalinaukas, Helen King: *Coaching – Realising the Potential*, IPD (London), 1994.

Carol Kennedy: *Guide to the Management Gurus*, Century Business Books, Random Century (London), 1991.

Herbert S Kindler: *Managing Disagreement Constructively*, Kogan Page (London), 1988.

Daniel T Kingsley: *How to Fire an Employee*, Facts on File Publications (New York), 1984.

Charles Margerison: Dick McCann: *Team Management*, Mercury Books (London), 1990.

Gerald Mars: *Cheats at Work – an anthology of workplace crime*, George Allen & Unwin (London), 1982.

Abraham Maslow: *Motivation and Personality*, Harper & Row (New York), 1970.

Douglas McGregor: *The Human Side of Enterprise*, McGraw Hill (New York), 1960; *The Professional Manager*, McGraw Hill (New York), 1967.

Ginny Nevill, Alice Pennicott, Joanna Williams, Ann Worrall: *Women in the Workforce – the effect of demographic changes in the 1990s*, The Industrial Society, (London), 1990.

Paddy O'Brien: *Taking the Macho out of Management*, Sheldon Press (London), 1993; *Positive Management Assertiveness for Managers*, Nicholas Brealey Publishing (London), 1992.

Tom Peters: *Thriving on Chaos*, Pan Books (London), 1989.

Edwin J Singer: *Effective Management Coaching*, IPM (London), 2nd edition, 1979.

Judy Skeats: *Successful Induction: how to get the most from your new employees*, Kogan Page (London), 1995.

Peter Stemp: *Are You Managing?*, the Industrial Society/Allied Dunbar Good Management Series (London), 1995.

Marilyn Wheeler: *Problem People at Work and How to Deal With Them*, Century Business Books, Random House (London), 1994.

Jerry Wisinski: *Resolving Conflicts on the Job*, American Management Association, Worksmart (New York), 1993.

John Whitmore: *Coaching for Performance*, Nicholas Brealey Publishing (London), 1992.

BIOGRAPHIES

Anita (consultant director) worked as a researcher in a professional institution and was promoted to management. She moved to publishing and, finally, management consultancy where she is now a senior director working internationally.

Beth (accountant) started work as a graduate trainee in one of the big six accountancy firms. Following a series of internal promotions and having a family, she took up an accountancy position in a Civil Service department.

Caroline (personnel manager) got her first job as a manager in an employers' association. She moved to Australia, working first for a consultancy, then moving to an international computer company. She has been promoted several times within this company and is back in England.

Diane (product manager) started work in a computer firm after university. She then moved to a major management consultancy, had children, and was promoted to be a product manager with European responsibility.

Emma (lawyer) has worked for 18 years for a large public service sector organization involved in administration of justice. She got a degree at Oxford and was called to the Bar, but took a junior legal post as it was better paid. She is now in senior management, responsible for 80 staff in a depressed inner city area.

Fiona (editor) started her career in publishing and took a career break to have a child. She then went to university and resumed her publishing career, starting as a writer before being promoted to editor.

Gail (training manager) started work in theatre administration, moving to local government personnel and then to training in a TV company. She has just started to set up as an independent trainer with colleagues.

Harriet (managing director) married young and had a family. She then went to university and decided to set up her own business. She is the managing director of a human resources consultancy.

Isobel (librarian) took history at Cambridge and postgraduate studies in librarianship. After a stint in a professional institute she moved to the City. She now manages a specialist library for a large, international finance firm.

Jean (chief executive) started her career as a nurse in the Royal Navy, later marrying and having children. She then took an Open University degree, liked writing and pursued a career in publishing, working in sales and editorial in several firms. When her company folded she went back to nursing for a while before setting up a recruitment agency with two other women and managing the business with this team for a few years. She returned to publishing but when the company went down, she found a backer and ran it herself but eventually it was forced to close. She applied for and got a chief executive's position in a promotional body.

Kim (civil servant) entered the Civil Service on the graduate entry scheme and worked in a range of government departments of different size and function and received a number of internal promotions. She then applied externally for a general manager's post in a public sector organization.

Linda (computer staff selection manager) worked as an accounts manager for a consultancy company which provides search and selection for companies needing computer staff. She was promoted after three years to become manager of a small department.

Margaret (biochemist) started in her biotechnology company after university. Through promotion she now holds the position of senior project leader.

Naomi (advertising director) got her first advertising management job in New Zealand after doing an early MBA. She moved to London and has worked for large multinationals in food manufacture and textiles and is currently with a service company.

Olivia (engineer) started her career in engineering on leaving university. Her husband worked for the same company and when he was transferred across the country she looked for a suitable post in the company so she could follow him and keep up her career. She moved to the new location, had a child and returned to work. She has been promoted in-company and now is a senior systems engineer.

Paula (finance controller) started as a graduate trainee in the public services (energy). After six years of rotations and promotions she moved to another large public service organization. She qualified as a chartered accountant and is now finance controller of the largest division of a manufacturing company.

Questa (manager in a trade association) worked in personnel research on leaving university and after a variety of jobs in research companies took up a management position in a trade association.

Ranee (doctor) chose community paediatrics as her speciality after medical school. She has worked as a junior doctor in numerous NHS hospitals as part of her training. She has risen to the level of senior registrar – the most senior level of junior doctor before a consultant's post.

Sarah (estate agent) left school before taking 'A' levels to follow her chosen career. She has worked in a variety of estate agencies – in the country and the town – moving to wherever her career took her. Her husband is in the same business and they have been able to coordinate their moves.

She now works for a property consultancy and has been promoted to become a director of the company.

Tania (research manager) worked in different fields of research (finance, industrial relations, sport). She has managed other researchers, reporters and advertising sales people and now works freelance.

Una (junior manager in retail) worked as a shop manager in a family-owned chain of newsagents before moving to a major retail chain store.

Vanessa (senior manager in public services) joined a large public sector organization on leaving university and has worked in a variety of increasingly senior roles in public services.

Wanda (lawyer/accountant) was originally a dancer. She put herself through legal and accountancy training and joined a multinational specifically to travel the world – and she does.

Xanthe (manager in entertainment industry) started as a secretary in the entertainment sector. She was promoted steadily over the years, rose to middle management and on retirement was begged to stay.

Yvonne and Zoe (junior managers in a professional institute) have limited managerial responsibilities. They have both combined work with bringing up children.